Normal for NORFOLK

KEITH SKIPPER

HALSGROVE

First published by Halsgrove in 2003

British Library Cataloguing-in-Publication Data
A CIP record for this title is available from the British Library

ISBN 1 84114 320 0

HALSGROVE
Halsgrove House
Lower Moor Way
Tiverton EX16 6SS
T: 01884 243242
F: 01884 243325
www.halsgrove.com

Printed in Great Britain by
The Cromwell Press, Trowbridge

Contents

Dedication

Dedicated to all Norfolk youngsters who claim it's a boring place and can't wait to get out. They will live and work elsewhere – yet still return as born-again locals ready to love it after all.

Acknowledgements

Thanks to all Norfolk friends and acquaintances – same thing in most cases – for feeding my production line so generously over the years.

Some articles, in part or whole, first appeared in the *Eastern Daily Press* or *Norfolk Journal*, and I am grateful to their respective editors, Peter Franzen and Pippa Bastin, for permission to feature them in this volume. Simon Butler of Halsgrove eagerly paved the way for this proudly parochial venture and gave me every encouragement to reach a wider audience.

My wife Diane yet again proved that my technological dyslexia need not be an automatic barrier to fame and fortune. She put all my words through the threshing machine, separating wholesome grain from scruffy husks.

We share the happy harvest.

Introduction

After more than forty years of writing and talking about my native county for a living, this is the proper time to take stock, to hand out a few home truths and to prove I have been paying attention most of the way.

All right, so there was that rather careless spell in the mid-1960s when I allowed my youthful adulation for the stars of Yarmouth's summer show firmament to take precedence over subtle but significant socio-economic changes on the seaside holiday scene. Who could possibly see Majorca pushing aside Morecambe (and Wise) or Corfu rivalling Caister, Cromer and other fashionable haunts along our coast?

Yes, I did take my eye off the farming ball in the early 1970s when Norwich City's soccer exploits soared to new heights and it was my job to say what it was like going to Wembley and Division One for the first time. Hardly surprising, then, that I should set aside the pastoral headlands for a few ninety-minute sporting acres while a trickle from the land threatened to turn into a flood and agri-business grew a fresh crop of custodians of the countryside looking more like merchant bankers.

And you don't see many of them on a bike.

Agreed, I should have paid a bit more attention throughout the 1980s as concrete mixers whirred, hard hats multiplied, new estates swallowed up whole meadows and increased traffic put a tremble in the trellis. But I was busy building a reputation as Norfolk's answer to Terry Wogan – even though no one had bothered even to pose the question.

Perhaps I might have seen posh writing on the old flint wall during an impromptu visit to Burnham Market on a nice day in the 1990s when a handsome but haughty woman brushed past to ask the shopkeeper how many sorts of extra virgin olive oil she stocked. It just didn't seem like a heavily loaded inquiry at the time.

Since the dawn of a brave new millennium – and some of us really doubted it would ever come to Norfolk – little has sneaked past me and my small team of border guards. It helps to be cunning. We have pointed several rich-and-famous evacuees from London looking for 'Chelsea-on-Sea' towards overspill settlements near Walberswick, Skegness and Southend. We have warned armies of potential developers that too many of the remaining greenfield sites in Norfolk are no more than hastily drained marshland where superior executive dwellings would surely sink without trace. We have cautioned mature people looking for retirement havens how lazy Norfolk winds and sharp indigenous eyes cut straight through you, especially in high summer. We have advised anyone angling for a slice of the rich tourism cake that it's about to go horribly stale through unexpected outbreaks of mad coypu disease.

Even so, we patriots cannot be everywhere, and a volume such as this offers a perfect opportunity to present an honest alternative to estate agent hyperbole, planning committee jargon, glossy magazine froth and clever-dick abuse from five-minute 'celebrities' who prove television hasn't so much dumbed down as gone completely subterranean.

Here is Norfolk, warts an' all, as surveyed by an unashamed son of the local soil who had mastered joined-up writing and spelling just as 'mechanisation', 'gentrification', 'colonisation', 'diversification' and 'spot the local' came into play. It dispels a few absurd myths about what is or is not 'Normal For Norfolk'.

For example, the Delia is not yet the official single currency – that idea was floated by the NIPs (Norfolk Independence Party) before the last General Election in the hope that all 16 tests could be met – but rolling pork cheeses along disused railway lines and well-undressing for hardy maidens on 15 January are still among futility rites retained on the calendar in various parts of the county.

This is an optimistic book written by someone who, when he says: 'I haven't lived anywhere else,' is making a proud boast and not a contrite confession. Norfolk does not need apologists. It deserves genuine respect and affection, not least for providing the Royal Family with a splendid country home (accessible to the public) and the rest of the capital with a perfect excuse to knock off early on Fridays.

Keith Skipper
Cromer, 2003

Prologue

Always shrewd, the Norfolk peasant is never tender; a wrong, real or imagined, rankles with him through a lifetime... Refinement of feeling he is quite incapable of.

Augustus Jessopp, scholar, writer and Rector of Scarning, 1890

Any political candidate who has addressed a Norfolk meeting will agree with me, I think, that the audience is slow to laugh, slower still in its reaction to pathos or indignation, and slowest of all in applause. But it may be this isolationist pride of them, and not stupidity at all... Norfolk people are at least sincere, they wear their demerits on the outside and their virtues within, so you are seldom taken in by them.

Doreen Wallace, Norfolk writer, 1951

If the rest of Britain sank beneath the waves, and Norfolk was left alone, islanded in the turmoil of the seas, it would, I think, survive without too much trouble... Norfolk has always stood alone and aloof from the rest of England.

James Wentworth Day, writer and broadcaster, 1976

Norfolk's population is now one of the fastest growing in the United Kingdom. Although this brings much-needed investment to what has been a rural backwater, it is all the more important that an awareness of the past should be the basis of planning for the future.

Susanna Wade Martins, Norfolk historian, 1988

1 *Road to Nowhere*

A Norfolk vicar, probably unaware that his calling would lead to missionary work in Antigua after the Second World War, summed up the county's glorious dilemma in his compelling hymn of praise composed in the 1920s. Frederick Oakley's verses, regulation issue for pining exiles as well as for natives clinging fast to home soil, included these lines still quoted freely by devotees and detractors alike:

> *It's on the road to Nowhere*
> *Travellers pass it by,*
> *Nobody comes to Norfolk*
> *Without a reason why.*

No change there, then, after three-quarters of a century! Sad old Norfolk, out on a limb with big, open skies and small, closed minds, implacably opposed to any kind of progress, chunter the critics.

Dear old Norfolk, bequeathed a wonderful brand of isolation by geography to shape real character and largely protect it, sigh the supporters.

Not much scope for common ground despite feelings of ambivalence given full expression by the big invasions led by trendy weekenders in recent years.

Norfolk has had to learn how generalisations can be dangerous as well as dismissive. Charles II claimed the place was fit only to be carved up for roads for the rest of the country. Horace Walpole pointed to the 'wilds of Norfolk' as districts to be shunned rather than sought out. Noel Coward didn't waste much dramatic feeling on his immortal line 'Very flat, Norfolk'. Had he bothered to ask, or taken a cycling holiday with the keep-fit cast of *Private Lives,* he would have discovered that, in altitude, the county ranges from 3 feet below sea level in Stow Bardolph Fen, near Downham Market, to 340 feet on the coastal reach at West Runton, between Cromer and Sheringham. There is some variety on the Road to Nowhere.

Very few variations, however, if you ask a stranger for a pen picture of what's on offer when you get there. Chances are you'll attract a mixture of Bernard Matthews' turkeys, Delia Smith's Canaries, The Singing Postman's rendition of the anthem 'Hev Yew Gotta Loight, Boy?' and a weak joke about Norfolk Broads being chatted up by yokels chewing straw and shaking pitchforks at Alan Partridge as he prances past with a ferret down his trousers. There might be a pot of mustard, a row of sugar beet or a restored windmill on a few lists, but Norfolk's general image does not alter much, thanks to stereotype fun and games.

Ironically, many of those all too ready to confuse traditional caution with calculated coldness, and comparative isolation with inbred ignorance, cannot camouflage their envy as they point accusing fingers at rustic dullards totally out of touch with the mainstream. Growing hordes of the worldly-wise and well-heeled seeking sanctuary in rural hideaways simply underline the double-edged attitude towards spots like Norfolk. Nice place – pity about the peasants and the potholes! Of course, some visitors can muster a sensitive approach and so provide a more discerning commentary as they slow down, marvel at the bracing air and wonder why it has taken so long to embark on this journey of enlightenment.

When he went *In Search of England* in 1927 – probably the last period when a metropolitan could visit his own country as he might a foreign land – H.V. Morton included the 'Land of the North Folk' on his tour. He found an England that 'warns us it is our duty to keep an eye on the old thatch because we may have to go back there some day, if not for the sake of our bodies, perhaps for the sake of our souls'.

Well, there's a fair bit of soul-searching going on right now, especially in North Norfolk's more fashionable quarters as urban dwellers stream towards flint cottages, weekend breaks, caravan parks, rambling safaris, bird-watching missions and pretty coastal resorts. If Morton predicted such a rolling tide, a movement increasingly threatening the very dream that inspires its followers, he also foresaw the likely reaction of the indigenous remnants:

> Norfolk is the most suspicious county in England. In Devon and Somerset men hit you on the back cordially; in Norfolk they look as though they would like to hit you over the head – till they size you up. You see, for centuries, the North Folk of East Anglia were accustomed to meet stray Vikings on lonely roads who had just waded ashore from the long boats.

'Good morning, bor!' said the Vikings. 'Which is the way to the church?'
'What d'ye want to know for?' was the Norfolk retort.
'Well, we thought about setting fire to it!'
*You will gather that Norfolk's suspicion of strangers, which is an
ancient complex bitten into the East Anglian through centuries of bit-
ter experience, is well grounded, and should never annoy the traveller.*

Rape and pillage, and setting fire to churches, may not be top of the
current invasion wish-list, but ugly developments, through-the-roof
house prices and gradual destruction of the spirit of a people and a
place are surely wicked affronts to Norfolk's precious 'dew diffrunt'
doctrine.

Modern Vikings, wading ashore with their Range Rovers, Agas,
Barbours, Puffas, stuffed olives, black truffles, green wellies and
the latest edition of 'How To Hack It In The Country' can be just as
dangerous as their horns-and-helmets predecessors. That's what a
venerable member of Burnham Market's 'ethnic minority' hinted
to me a year or so back when I presented an evening of local entertainment in the village hall. Some called it timely missionary work.

The sage's colourful summary of life in the village at the heart of
'Chelsea-on-Sea' went something like this. I have ironed out and
phonetically modified a few of his broader words and phrases:

*We dunt harf get some rum'uns round here. There's the posh set who
talk proper with a plum in thar mouths and look down thar noses at
evrawun else. There's them who try ter talk proper an' pretend ter be suffin' they arnt, an' there's them who dunt add up to a sight whatever they
dew or say. There's a tidy few who move inter the village an' muck in.
There's another tidy few who never git orff thar backsides ter join in anything. O'corse they're the ones who moan the loudest 'bowt village life
fallin' apart. Glad ter say we dew still hev the backbone brigade, people
who keep places like this (the village hall) goin' so we hev a regular place
ter meet an' mardle. There ent enough real locals ter go round, so some
o'them newcomers (resident for less than twenty years) help out. I dun
my bit afore this part o' Norfolk went all trendy, an' I spooz my favourite
pastime now is watchin' and listenin' while that smart set swan about as
if they own the place. Rich weekenders dunt want a half o' mild an' a
quiet game o'cribbage...'*

More amusement than anguish in his voice, although I'm sure
he knew he represented the fast-dwindling old guard of backwater

existence. His descriptions, beautifully biased in favour of the parochial flag rather than wider economic implications, could easily be applied to countless other Norfolk communities where new money, new people and new ways have made telling marks. The seven Burnhams, Holkham, Brancaster, Stiffkey, Morston, Blakeney, Cley and Holt just happen to be at the well-advertised heart of this gentrification empire where being out on a geographical limb merely renders discovery and exploration all the more enticing.

Yes, there are obvious economic windfalls, especially if you run a smart shop, delicatessen, hotel, restaurant, or art gallery – and life has its uplifting moments for poor, downtrodden estate agents desperate to become prophets of boom. (As I write this halfway through 2003, my Norfolk bush telegraph points to Docking as next likely property hotspot, 6 miles south-west of Burnham Market, 13 miles west of Wells, 17 miles north-east of King's Lynn and 117 miles and a bit from London as the commuter flees).

With tiny cottages selling for around £200,000 as an ideal weekend bolt-hole for a capital lawyer, it comes as no staggering surprise to find local folk priced off the property ladder. Indeed, social ramifications go much deeper than the long-running debate over whether second homes should pay full council tax. Local authorities seem unable or unwilling to do very much against the celebrity swing to magnetic north.

Many locals described as 'insulting' a campaign to persuade London-based weekend cottage owners to rent their Norfolk hide-aways to the local home seekers. North Norfolk District Council went so far as to place adverts in the *London Evening Standard*. After 50 replies, three home owners are reported to have signed up to deals securing them guaranteed incomes – a pinprick on the conscience of those who want to make a real dent in the area's affordable housing problem.

That gesture of a venture pales even more into insignificance alongside rousing fanfares reserved for the latest celebrity to call for some well-deserved peace and quiet.

Former Prime Minister John Major and his wife Norma celebrated the dawn of a new millennium by buying a second home at Weybourne, near Sheringham, planning to split their time between Huntingdon and the new pad. The five-bedroom 1950s home set in 12 acres and in need of extensive renovations would be 'much more than a holiday retreat. Our family and friends will come and stay with us there. Anyone who thinks we are going to use it as a two-week holiday home is utterly wrong' affirmed the Major manifesto.

He went for a bonus point by revealing he had been evacuated to Norfolk as a baby during the Second World War. 'I think the North Norfolk coast is lovely and I can move between Huntingdon and Norfolk in under two hours. I love the coastline, there are some charming places in Norfolk and there are some really great shops.' And just one more little point worth making, 'Rather like Cambridgeshire, there are some really friendly people.'

A part-time return about sixty years after his evacuation was marked by round-the-clock security (paid for eventually by the Home Office) and the latest round of speculation over who would be next to exchange fleshpots for crab pots, gridlocked streets for lonely creeks, Canary Wharf for Holkham Hall.

Steady, now! I must take extra care not to sound like a cross between a poetic estate agent and an excitable tourism official. After all, we can't have that Road to Nowhere being loved to death – even by those who can afford to give it a long and impeccably organised funeral.

∾

NORFOLK

HYMN OF PRAISE BY NORFOLK RECTOR
FREDERICK OAKLEY

God drew the map of England,
He planted hill and wood,
He looked on stream and headland,
And saw that it was good.

Pushed far into a corner,
He left a fair domain,
Heath, down, and fen, and ploughland,
Rich pasturage and grain.

It's on the road to Nowhere
Travellers pass it by,
Nobody comes to Norfolk,
Without a reason why.

Nobody sings of Norfolk,
Though many bards there be
To honour glorious Devon,
Or Sussex by the sea.

When God made Norfolk County,
He said they'd love her well
Who, patient in her wooing
Surrendered to her spell.

Slowly she charms, how slowly,
But once the spell is cast
By Norfolk on her lovers,
She holds them to the last.

Norfolk's a stately lady
She'll keep aloof for years,
'Furriners' she despises,
She's scornful of the 'Sheers'.

But they'll not hold her fickle
Who once her true love win.
From Brancaster to Thetford,
From Caister to King's Lynn.

We're slow of speech in Norfolk,
Perhaps a thought too slow,
And only when we're cornered
We'll answer 'Yes' or 'No'.

Our Fathers taught us caution
They learned with moil and pain
That every Precious stranger
Might be a thieving Dane.

The sturdy Norfolk yeoman
To guard their rights are set
As well befits the children
Of men who followed Kett.

Yet Norfolk men are loyal,
Without deceit or sham,
Ask, if you think it doubtful
The 'Squire of Sandringham'.

Devon may boast her sailors,
But Norfolk holds the claim
To lead all other counties
By right of Nelson's name.

And mark in France and Flanders,
And far beyond the waves,
The thousand wooden crosses
Guarding our Norfolk graves.

When God made Norfolk County
He showed this perfect art,
Within her fair, proud body
He hid a golden heart.

So come and live in Norfolk
Bide, till her spell is cast,
Then, once you've learned to love her,
You'll love her to the last.

෨෩

2 Rail to Somewhere

As dark mutterings multiply at the way rich and famous incomers totally change the character of 'old Norfolk', particularly in and around Burnham Market, it may be worth calling for order and presenting a short history lesson. Yes, we have seen and heard it all before.

A burning desire to get away from it all is nothing new. The Victorians were just as much caught up in the hunt for peaceful haunts where they could unwind and let the pressures of life's increasing pace and demands gently soak away. For the wealthy that could mean a long and arduous trip to the Jura mountains or Swiss lakes. To the less well-off, it brought a trip to bracing Margate or some other seaside resort. For many it was a Bank Holiday outing to the coast just for the day.

So, a little over a century ago, by which time almost every part of England could be reached by train, railway companies vied with each other to promote new branch lines to rural backwaters. In the mid-1880s an intriguing fresh name appeared on colourful billboards around main London stations advertising a place called Poppyland. It looked most appealing, but where was it, why was it so called and why go there anyway?

Well, readers of the *Daily Telegraph* would not have been mystified. They were well versed in the fulsome articles of Clement Scott, the paper's theatre critic and travel writer. He thought up the romantic name of Poppyland after a routine assignment to write about the new extension of the Great Eastern Railway Company's line to the North Norfolk coast. Up to 1882 the line had finished at Norwich. The following August, Scott travelled up on the new line from London to Cromer – and Norfolk's recent history as a tourist attraction might have been very different had the distinguished journalist taken more of a liking to the little fishing port.

More used to the fashionable watering holes of Continental attractions like Baden-Baden or Evian, Scott turned his back on the boisterous families and crowded sands to embark on a stroll out of town southwards along the cliff edge. One of the most fateful walks in the history of tourism in this country took him inland, attracted by the ruin of an old church tower and the distant view of a tiny hamlet. Scott was entranced as he wrote:

> *It is difficult to convey an idea of the silence of the fields through which I passed, or the beauty of the prospect that surrounded me – a blue sky without a cloud across it; a sea sparkling under a haze of heat; wild flowers in profusion around me, poppies predominating everywhere...*

Come on, Clement, feed our jaded imaginations some more as we sit at our Victorian breakfast tables and wait to be lured to pastures new:

> *Looking across the fields there was no sound but the regular click of the reaping machine under which the golden grain was falling. It was just the time of day when an English farm has such a sleepy look. No one seemed about anywhere as I surveyed the farm buildings, no voice broke the silence...*

Enter prize Norfolk extras, the miller and his nineteen-year-old brighteyed daughter. Louie Jermy was wrapped in plain country clothes and a bonnet trimmed with poppies. They lived in a farmhouse – 'the exact reproduction of the style of cottage that all children are set to draw when they commence their first lesson' – next to an old windmill.

Louie was dubbed The Maid of the Mill by other writers destined to follow Scott on his pilgrimage to Poppyland. After settling in, Scott roamed the lanes and was only two fields away from strolling on a deserted beach. He could swim in the sea without another soul in sight. 'Had I been cast on a desert island I could not have been more alone.'

The old church tower on the cliff by the sea continued to draw him, and he immortalised the place in his poem 'The Garden of Sleep', later published in his book, *Poppyland Papers*. He tried to disguise the identity of the nearby village in his eagerly awaited newspaper columns during the following weeks by calling it Beckhythe, but that only seemed to increase the magnetism of the place in the minds of his million or so readers. Of course, all the curious had to do was retrace the steps he had taken and look for an abundance of poppies.

So began the Poppyland legend and an inevitable invasion of artistic and influential notables to the small settlements of Overstrand and

Sidestrand. It remains to be seen if the Chelsea-on-Sea phenomenon makes as deep an imprint on the Norfolk social picture, but certain parallels can be drawn already. The written word remains a potent tool.

Glossy magazines, sensing the time to be right for discovering alternatives to Suffolk's celebrity hot spots at Southwold and Aldeburgh, all beach huts and Benjamin Britten, found the perfect capital for a new must-visit empire not far away. Burnham Market, soon rechristened Burnham Upmarket, fitted snugly into that role, Georgian houses sitting around a church and village green with a small stream running through. Had Clement Scott got this far on his first visit in 1883, who is to say he wouldn't have brought forward the rise of the Norfolk Riviera here by a century or so? I reckon he would have made much more of Lord Nelson's birthplace at Burnham Thorpe than his modern counterparts, although the locals, understandably, are extremely grateful it has not been turned into a tatty, souvenir-spattered shrine to Norfolk's favourite son and one of this country's most durable heroes.

Personalities descending on Poppyland had, in the main, more substance and sophistication than the bulk of television charmers and celebrity chefs floating around the delicatessens, restaurants, hotels and specialist shops at the heart of Chelsea-on-Sea. A quick glance at a lengthy list of eminent callers towards the end of the nineteenth century reveals several names still carrying considerable weight today – poet Algernon Charles Swinburne; writer Theodore Watts-Dunton; first knight of the theatre Sir Henry Irving; Shakespearean actress supreme Dame Ellen Terry; publisher Andrew Chatto; actor-manager Sir Herbert Beerbohm-Tree and his equally famous daughter, Viola. Such was the society in which Clement Scott moved, and these and many others headed for Poppyland as a result of his beckoning.

Many unusual happenings came to pass in the hitherto quiet countryside. George R. Sims, who wrote a famous column, Mustard and Cress, for *The Referee* was often a guest of the Jermys, at Mill House. On one occasion Sims roamed around Overstrand after spreading the news that he was a lunatic and that his companion, the actor Henry Petit, was his keeper. Then there was the time when Sims bought all the home-made blackberry jam from the now celebrated hostess at Mill House, knowing that Scott was most partial to it and was due in a few days. Ghostly rattlings and murderous cries around the lanes late at night could usually be attributed to Sims and his cronies.

A building boom, with impressive mansions shooting up, was led by Lord and Lady Battersea. Overstrand became known as The Village of

Millionaires. Poppyland souvenir industries blossomed. Poppyland china, from candle holders to full tea services, was sold in local shops, and Daniel Davison, a Cromer chemist and photographer, produced Poppyland Bouquet. This was principally a perfume, although soap was also made. The perfume was sold worldwide and made until 1930, based on a French spirit and using 15 other ingredients. The Great Eastern Railway produced scores of Poppyland posters to encourage folk to use their service to visit North Norfolk. Publications multiplied and postcards were produced by the thousand. Poppyland spread its petals way beyond Overstrand and Sidestrand.

Clement Scott, as its discoverer and main champion, remained the doyen of its visitors. He continued to make the journey there for fifteen years, not only in summer but also in midwinter. He penned 'The Garden of Sleep' while standing in the churchyard by the old church tower at Christmas, 1885, and it was a special ritual of his to travel there and see in the New Year from the same spot, reading his poem as a reminder of the first days of his discovery and, in some ways, as a lament for what his publicity had done. Scott died in 1904. He lived to see his rural haven of peace turned into what he called Bungalowland.

There's no denying the massive influence he exerted on this part of the county, although it is fascinating to note there was little appreciation for his efforts shortly after his death. In its edition of 12 September 1909, the *North Norfolk News* reported latest proceedings at Cromer Council. One Captain Smith, secretary to the Metropolitan Drinking Fountain and Cattle Trough Association, had written again to the council concerning the siting of a 'fountain', a memorial to the late Clement Scott. The council was far from unanimous in supporting its coming to Cromer, and one member suggested it had been 'hurled at them'. Another member doubted that it should be referred to as a fountain when, in fact, it was a cattle drinking trough. 'Unfortunately,' continued Captain Smith in his letter, 'the fountain and trough has already been dispatched, with the inscription placed on it.'

It can be seen today at what many regard as the entrance to Poppyland, at the junction of the Overstrand and Northrepps Roads. The inscription reads:

To Clement Scott, who by his pen immortalised *'Poppyland'*; erected by many friends, November, 1909.

A drinking trough may seem a rather lacklustre memorial to the man who thought up the name Poppyland and made the district so fashionable. But I sense he would have been embarrassed by anything too extravagant, bearing in mind his regrets at the marvellous advertising job he had done.

One doubts if any such qualms are afflicting either those who beat a regular path to the Burnhams or the purveyors of purple prose encouraging them to do so. There's no one outstanding Clement Scott-type figure at the helm of this highly effective publicity drive, so a drinking trough salute to the darling days of Chelsea-on-Sea seems unlikely when another trendy corner beckons.

Perhaps a champagne bottle with ice bucket bobbing up and down in that Burnham Market stream will serve as a fitting memorial. When the bubble bursts.

∽

THE GARDEN OF SLEEP
(By Clement Scott, 1841–1904)

On the grass of the cliff, at the edge of the steep,
God planted a garden – a garden of sleep!
'Neath the blue of the sky, in the green of the corn,
It is there that the regal red poppies are born!
Brief days of desire, and long dreams of delight,
They are mine when my Poppyland cometh in sight.
In music of distance, with eyes that are wet,
It is there I remember, and there I forget!
O! heart of my heart! Where the poppies are born
I am waiting for thee, in the hush of the corn.
Sleep! Sleep! From the Cliff to the Deep!
Sleep, my Poppyland Sleep!

In my garden of sleep, where red poppies are spread,
I wait for the living, alone with the dead!
For a tower in ruin stands guard o'er the deep,
At whose feet are green graves of dear women asleep!
Did they love as I love, when they lived by the sea?
Did they wait as I wait for the days that may be?
Was it hope or fulfilling that entered each breast,
Ere death gave release, and the poppies gave rest?
O! life of my life! on the cliffs by the sea,
By the graves in the grass, I am waiting for thee
Sleep! Sleep! In the Dews by the Deep!
Sleep, my Poppyland, Sleep!

3 *Snipers' Bullets*

For some of us, one of Norfolk's most endearing little habits is to pay homage to all the latest fads, to embrace the true spirit of progress in which they are wrapped – and then to quietly shuffle along the same old homely track.

Critics call it self-delusion. I prefer to see it as a shrewd tactic at the core of a self-preservation programme designed to fend off constant demands to 'move with the times', voiced mainly by those with vested interests in items Norfolk can well do without ... like motorways, mass tourism projects, more sprawling estates and towering, glowering masts mucking up our glorious skyline. Such a radical approach does have its hazards, not least when jibes about being out of touch, ignoring the inevitable and falling victim to rampant nostalgia degenerate swiftly into vitriolic abuse.

Some of my best friends suggest I live on the battlements of 'Fortress Norfolk', eager to repel all bringers of enlightenment to a comparatively dark land. Such summary judgement could be based on an occasional refusal to clamber aboard the latest express roaring across the communications superhighway. I do not drive a car. I do not own a mobile phone. I shun satellite television. I prefer joined-up writing for personal letters. I am an exception to the rule, but that's a proud Norfolk trait worthy of some applause, surely, instead of immediate condemnation. I'm amazed at the number of people who secretly admire old-fashioned renegades, but do not find it expedient to say so in public!

They prefer to remind us how we ought to be flattered so many others want to come and live among us, to sample the beauties of one of the last outposts of civilisation. They preach the same old sermon about Norfolk being such a big place, it can take anything the developers can throw at it and yet retain its essential charm. Resistance is futile, however colourfully or coherently it might be presented, so it must make sense to take full advantage of what's on offer. It cuts no ice with such folk when you suggest the resistance movement forms the campaigning conscience of a reluctant population – a fast-growing population – most of whom will be only too pleased to grab all the benefits without bothering to give a second thought to any of the consequences of rapid development.

At least these sparring sessions are carried out in a reasonably amiable climate, with agreements to differ accepted with equal magnanimity. Norfolk's ability to laugh at itself, weaned on centuries of silly generalisations about more remote corners of a shrinking world, clearly helps to keep the peace. Unfortunately, it doesn't end there. All too often in more recent times, Norfolk has been forced to endure cheap and nasty jeering from smart metropolitans firing away from a safe distance.

Jeremy Clarkson, a television presenter and motoring pundit who gives the art of abuse some very fine tuning, clearly relished his self-appointed role as basher-in-chief. I recall a 1993 article from the heart in which he dismissed Norfolk as a flat and featureless county littered with yokels, perverts and cretins:

> *They spend millions telling us that it is foolish to smoke but not a penny telling you not to go to Norfolk – unless you like orgies and the ritual slaying of farmyard animals.*

Mr Clarkson revved up some more, classing the county as impossible to get to. (So how could he come to any conclusions?) And no one there understood cars:

> *I am used to having people point as I go by. Most shout, 'Hey, look it's a Cosworth!!', but in Norfolk they shout, 'Hey, look, it's a car!'*

Rollicking humour from a super-charged ego, and we were treated to several more of his subtle tirades on the so-called entertainment circuit.

Perhaps he was inspired by a notorious attack launched on the arts pages of the *Sunday Telegraph* in 1991. Prolific writer A.N. Wilson, a Fellow of the Royal Society of Literature, turned his exceptional talents to sizing up the week's television programmes under the heading: 'Mad but Normal for Norfolk.' Out of his disappointment for a play with a rural setting he contrived this vicious summary:

> *I know of a medical practice in rural East Anglia where the majority of the patients are inbred, hare-lipped, mental defectives. When they*

put their boot faces round the surgery door and pour out their tales of woe to the doctor, the GP writes 'N.F.N.' on their notes. It means 'Normal for Norfolk'. As well as being very flat, Norfolk is full of curmudgeonly human monsters. Tucked away in their bleak villages beneath the large threatening skies, they are still as belligerent as they were in the days of Queen Boadicea.

Then he decided this 'miserable play' under review had some merit after all, serving as 'a useful antidote for anyone watching it who might be tempted as yuppies in the 1980s used to be, by the idea of a second home in some Norfolk village where property, like human life, is cheap.' Clearly, he had not ventured as far as Burnham Market.

Still, anger and pity had to give way to a measure of grudging gratitude for making would-be settlers think carefully before throwing in their lot with belligerent peasants in bleak villages under threatening skies. I don't know of any specific reason why Mr Wilson (Rugby; New College, Oxford; born in Staffordshire and raised in Wales) should dip his pen into so much acid – and he didn't see fit to reply to my curt but polite letter of inquiry at the time – but the need to sell newspapers, even in the 'quality' arena, should not excuse such grubby blanket condemnation of an entire county.

Of course, some suggest it is foolish to rise to the bait, to waste time trying to counter such ill-conceived comments. Trouble is, silence can be interpreted as meek acquiescence – an obvious affront to the reputation of belligerent peasants gradually mastering the art of opening a paper without too many pictures, and recognising an insult when they read one. Education has a lot to answer for.

We don't take too kindly to those infuriatingly broad surveys apparently carried out simply to raise Norfolk blood pressures and posh magazines' circulations. One of the most blatantly contrived sweeps branded Norfolk the most unfriendly county in the United Kingdom, along with Yorkshire, while Mileham was singled out for the title of worst village in the country for accepting newcomers. This survey took in only a sample of parishes across the United Kingdom and the in-depth researcher admitted she had not spoken to anyone in Suffolk or Cambridgeshire. Nor was it made clear how the whole business had been conducted among Norfolk natives and newcomers. After all, it is important what you ask, how you ask it and who is invited to give answers.

As a footnote, the magazine did have the decency to suggest Norfolk was more likely to accept newcomers if they took an active part in village life. Well, I would consider that a reasonable sort of rule to apply anywhere in these fast-changing times.

Magazines spattered with hyphens, hyperbole and titles shouldn't be taken too seriously when they dip well-formed toes into untested waters. But again, it seems perfectly reasonable to complain, preferably in a broad Norfolk accent, when distorted images are all we can see reflected as a result.

Good-natured ribbing is an accepted part of Norfolk life. We find an element of admiration in back-handers like one issued by a previous Bishop of Norwich: 'The only way to lead Norfolk people is first to find out which way they are going – and then march in front of them.' It is one thing to be noticed for being different, and to be gently chastised for it on occasions, but Norfolk diehards draw the line at being told to apologise unreservedly for following natural instincts.

Adding injury to insults over the years has been persistent misrepresentation of the way Norfolk people speak, particularly in television and radio productions with a Norfolk setting. These make a mockery of geography, local pride and artistic accuracy as we are portrayed as a little place wedged somewhere between Devon and Dorset. The locals mutter 'oooooooh-aaaaaaaaaah! Oooooooooh-aaaaaaaaaah!' a bit like a West Country ambulance going full pelt.

Arnold Wesker, who put Norfolk on an international stage with his play *Roots*, apologised to me many times for the way our county is mocked by the 'Mummerzet' brigade. His own work has suffered from blatantly bogus bucolic tones, and he was delighted to welcome the formation of Friends Of Norfolk Dialect (FOND) in 1999 to help shine much-needed light on murky corners. We were fortunate to land as our president Professor Peter Trudgill, a figure of international repute in his field. Born and brought up in Norwich, he became Professor of English Linguistics at the University of Fribourg in Switzerland. As FOND flourished, he emphasised:

One of the biggest cultural catastrophes facing the modern world is the loss of languages. Some estimates suggest that as many as 90 per cent of the 6000 or so languages in the world are in danger of extinction in the next 100 years. Parallel to this loss of languages, and in many ways just as frightening, is the loss of dialectical diversity… Very often people stop speaking their local dialect, or fail to pass it on to their children, because they feel it is inferior, inadequate and something to be ashamed of. In FOND we know that the English dialect of Norfolk is part of a long tradition that can be studied in our schools and elsewhere. It is an expressive, rich, distinctive and useful language variety that is part of a wider patchwork of English local dialects that makes our language so varied and interesting.

His sentiments were echoed by Norfolk MP and former Education Secretary Gillian Shephard as she joined the chorus in praise of the preservation of this strand of Norfolk's cultural heritage. So it is clear how genuine support stretches way beyond the 'charming anachronism' level, and it is not confined to the indigenous population. Newcomers and visitors show keen interest – and there are a few encouraging signs that producers of national television and radio plays featuring the county are trying to capture the authentic sound.

Meanwhile, we brace ourselves for more sad little salvos aimed at brooding peasants with pointed heads who marry close relatives and play 'I spy with my middle eye' under threatening skies.

How strange so many smart incomers want to risk time in their belligerent company!

4 *Fond Farewells*

Over half a century ago, I sat reading the Bible to my grandmother. She was blind, and children of our big family living nearby took it in turn to read to her, with a Sunday dinner as the reward.

I must have impressed on this occasion – probably pronouncing Leviticus correctly – because as I finished and asked if we were having batter puddings, she told me I ought to give serious thought to becoming a parson. I was about eight and didn't think much of the idea. I wanted to be another Hopalong Cassidy or Len Hutton, so I wasn't prepared to make any pledges to go into the pulpit. Grandmother had the perfect incentive to counter such doubts, 'Just you think of all the nice things you can say about people at funerals!' she beamed.

I didn't take holy orders, from her or anybody else, but I reflect on that little Sunday dinnertime episode every time I'm invited to say a few words at fond farewells to old friends and colleagues. Affection and thanksgiving rather than theology have provided the sort of opportunities my dear old grandmother had in mind. I recall with particular pride passing on a few warming thoughts at the December funerals of my inspirational village schoolteacher, Marjorie Tann, and my first sports editor and drama-loving colleague, Ted Bell.

I have also been in a privileged position for over two decades to fashion little salutes towards countless characters who have left the Norfolk scene, using either the local airwaves at Radio Norfolk or my regular weekly page in the *Eastern Daily Press.*

Here are just a few tributes to members of that colourful Norfolk congregation. Gone but not forgotten…

JOE JORDAN

The Grand Old Man of the Marshes has found his eternal creek.

A mite fanciful, perhaps, for such a down-to-earth Norfolk character, but Joe Jordan couldn't help but inspire that sort of poetic flight.

He died well into his ninety-first year after a lifetime of perfecting the old trick of having one foot on the land and the other in the sea. He could have called his memoirs Boots and Boats.

Joe was as much a part of the small coastal village of Stiffkey as the flint cobbles and old red brick that combine so handsomely to make it a magnet for settlers and visitors.

Born here in 1912, one of 13 children, he knew it when hard graft and self-sufficiency were cornerstones of local life. He remained true to these virtues as Stiffkey, like so much of North Norfolk, went with the tide of rich second-homers and smartly clad roamers.

I savoured several lengthy mardles with Joe as he grew old gratefully. He exuded good humour, rude health and obvious gratitude for roles allotted him over the years, sixty-nine of them alongside his proud wife, Winnie.

From crow-scaring to driving a combine, he worked the land in and around Stiffkey until retirement at sixty-five. He was released from the farm for three months of the year to watch over the nesting birds for the Nature Conservancy Council.

As an auxiliary coastguard for nearly thirty years, he saved dozens of lives – even though he couldn't swim – and was made an MBE in 1978 for rescue and conservation work. Two years earlier, Joe had been presented with an RNLI bronze medal for rescuing two men on the marshes.

He knew those marshes intimately, packed with magic and menace in equal measure, as he collected cockles, mussels, winkles and samphire and maintained a constant vigil for the welfare of wildlife and humans alike.

BRYAN STEVENS

Old friend and colleague Bryan Stevens preached what he had practised as a cricketer of note.

We worked together on the *Eastern Daily Press* sports desk in the 1970s where he forgave many of my youthful excesses because we shared a common passion for the great summer game.

Bryan, whose wonderful Norfolk innings ended at the age of eighty-one, always played a straight bat where others indulged in fancy dabs or dangerous sweeps. He cut his *Wisden* teeth and marked his crease in an era when 'playing the game' was an automatic virtue rather than a quaint left-over.

After playing for the county with distinction, like his father before him, Bryan reported on Norfolk's fortunes without frills as 'facts and figures speak for themselves'.

Bryan smoked a pipe, wore braces, rode a bike and kept the sensible haircut in vogue. He despised the rise of sports' barmy armies, on and off the field.

I recall a mid-wicket conference in Norwich's London Street a few seasons after our newspaper partnership had ended. Bryan pointed earnestly to the growing trend of cricketers wearing floppy hats as an inevitable lever for more sloppy behaviour.

Yes, he was old-fashioned, but also knowledgeable, thoughtful, loyal and splendid company over a pint. He will be welcome in that Great Pavilion in the Sky. Thatched, of course.

SIR ARTHUR SOUTH

My dealings with Sir Arthur South were based mainly around the Norwich City football scene of the 1970s.

As the club chairman, trying to make sense of an increasingly volatile business, he relished sparring sessions with 'the gentlemen of the press – or perhaps I'll call you scribes and Pharisees!'

I knew him well enough to feel comfortable when invited to continue calling him plain Arthur following his knighthood, and we shared after-dinner speaking duties at many local functions.

On one occasion he rang me at the *Eastern Daily Press* sports desk in the afternoon in search of a few details about a cricket club we were both toasting that evening.

He batted first – and turned my smattering of facts and figures into a 45-minute eulogy that convinced everyone present he had followed the club passionately for at least three decades.

Like so many political opponents he had demolished over the years, I was left virtually speechless – but still in awe of a masterful performer.

For all the bluster and well-practised rhetoric, Arthur had an extremely sensitive side, a trait painfully exposed when his personal life was trawled out for public inspection by national tabloid tormentors.

His key strengths included the ability to laugh at himself and so take the sting out of pressure situations. There were plenty of these during his spell at the Carrow Road helm, not least when fellow 'hard man' on Saunders felt like mixing it.

My favourite memory, however, goes back to the after-dinner circuit. Arthur was in full flow amid the cigar smoke and sporting bonhomie. Suddenly, a waitress dropped a tin tray behind the top table. The clang brought Arthur to a halt.

He turned and asked with mock politeness if the good woman would like to stay and listen quietly to the rest of his oration.

'No thankyer,' she replied curtly, 'I git enough o' that ole squit at hoom.'

Arthur led the spontaneous applause as she made a dramatic exit.

'SHRIMP' DAVIES

I came late under the spell of Henry 'Shrimp' Davies, lifeboat legend and twinkling mardler.

He had been home from the sea as Cromer coxswain for over a decade by the time I moved to the town in 1988. 'Welcome to the coast, boy – and don't go out there when the water's lumpy!'

We met regularly on the promenade for a Sunday morning gossip. Shrimp mixed memories and character sketches with pithy comments on current topics. He was responsible for the best Norfolk riposte in my collection.

'We get some rum'uns round here, don't we?' he teased. I played the game and asked what he meant.

'Chap came up to me in Jetty Street the other day and started slagging off the place... "Blooming Cromer, it's the backside of Norfolk," he growled.'

What on earth did he say to that?

I looked him straight in the eye and said, "Oh, yes, and are you just passing through?"'

LES POTTER

Les Potter was well into his political stride by the time I became a young newspaper reporter in Dereham in the early 1960s.

His strong personality and attachment to so many local organisations and issues made him an influential figure at most important meetings I attended. I was warned not to let him dominate every story, however hard it might be to ignore a colourful flood of quotable quotes.

One of his keen rivals complained regularly that the bulk of his own telling comments had been squeezed out at the expense of yet another 'Potter paroxysm of agonised sincerity'.

Another would visit the press office almost every week to berate me for not putting in the paper what he had said. He seemed less than placated by my suggestion that he ought to be grateful for such an omission.

Les, of course, played a shrewder game. He never complained, not even when choppy waters of controversy threatened to engulf him. He invited reporters to The Bull pub next door for a drink.

'That's for putting in the paper what I meant to say!' he chortled.
Can it be any wonder he lasted so long on the Norfolk public stage?

BRIAN BOWLE

The death at ninety-three of my old chemistry master Brian Bowle
will spark countless yarns among former pupils of Hamond's
Grammar School at Swaffham.

Mr Bowle, known affectionately as Chad as he peered over his lab-
oratory desk at the world of test tubes and Bunsen burners, taught at
the school from 1946 until 1967, including a spell as deputy headmas-
ter. He was also a leading figure on the local music scene.

Chad's benevolent streak was sorely tested by pupils like me who
couldn't say 'hydrolysis', let alone explain what it meant.

One of the most embarrassing incidents of my ill-starred chemistry
career concerned a mark of 14 per cent for a surprise written exami-
nation. Chad was deeply suspicious of this sudden improvement in
my performance.

Sadly, such misgivings were well founded. The litmus test was
checking the paper of the boy next to me. It revealed uncanny resem-
blances, including a very strange spelling of 'highdrollersis'.

CLIFF TEMPLE

Cliff Richard Temple – and how he chuckled when you emphasised
the first two names – was the Peter Pan of Norfolk photography.

It all began with a Box Brownie in the 1920s as a Yarmouth lad
enthused over scenes he dearly wanted to share. His passion developed into one of the biggest personal archives in the area.

Cliff, who died at ninety-two, was no dry hoarder of history. He
was generous to a fault in allowing local and national publications to
use his pictures at no more cost than an acknowledgement.

He also compiled splendid books of his own, with wherries
and windmills, shipwrecks and show business and herring and
horses just a few of the topics on a crowded canvas stretching over
seventy years.

Our last meeting came a few days before Christmas 1998 as carols
rang out at Priscilla Bacon Lodge in Norwich. Cliff held court up the
corner, a craggy, defiant figure, still inquisitive and ready to prove the
old grey matter had a few mardles to go.

'Chances are I shan't see the next century,' he mused with scarcely
a hint of regret. I suggested he had done his bit to help us remember
the present one.

JIM HOLMES

My last mardle with Jim Holmes covered a lot of ground. He thanked me for writing a foreword for his book, *Apple Man*, the story of his colourful years selling home-grown products direct to the public on Yarmouth Market.

Jim died at eighty-four just as his new book was published, a fitting memorial to an effervescent character who leaves distinctive marks on Yarmouth, Gorleston and the surrounding Flegg villages.

He cultivated an intriguing chronicle out of that little Ormesby plot where he started work alongside Kathleen, a willing and thrifty wife, soon after the Second World War. They rolled up their sleeves and toiled long hours for small rewards, never afraid to diversify in the name of survival.

Shrewd observation and a lively sense of humour were Jim's other ready companions for more than thirty years as a stallholder on Yarmouth Market. The book features a rich cavalcade of personalities from racing tipster Prince Monolulu to the Big Drips, who couldn't see as far as the end of their noses.

I remain amazed that Jim found time to immerse himself in so many other matters outside his immediate field. He gave talks on Parson James Woodforde, National Trust buildings, Norwich Cathedral, the Yarmouth Fisherman's Hospital and about a score of other 'specialist subjects'.

GEOFFREY DIMOCK

My old history master kept one significant date very much to himself. Now we know why.

Geoffrey Dimock, who taught at Hamond's Grammar School from 1950 until 1974, died after a long and lively retirement. He would have reached ninety on 1 April 2002.

Hardly surprising that he kept birthday details well hidden from impish schoolboys for whom such a revelation would have triggered an overflow of japes and titters.

Not that 'Mr Bim' lacked humour. He encouraged a cheerful response to serious questions about Napoleon extinguishing himself on the battlefield. He was known to be easily sidetracked from the Unification of Italy to Norwich City's promotion hopes or England's Test chances at Trent Bridge.

Indeed, sport played a big part in his life, both at school and when his teaching career ended. Cricket, golf, snooker and bridge kept him to the fore in and around Swaffham. We enjoyed many happy reunions at Old Hamondians' events where he apologised regularly to my wife for being partly responsible for the way I had turned out.

In fact, Mr Dimock helped push my education to unexpected heights. I returned to Hamond's in the autumn of 1960 without a job or any clear sense of direction. He saw me skulking outside a class-room, 'making the place look untidy', and turned compassion into immediate action.

He engineered the chance for me to go 'on probation' in the sixth form to pursue the only subjects for which I had shown an obvious aptitude. The rest, as they say, is history and English, a two-year extension which taught me hard work could be rewarding and fun.

GEORGE JESSUP

Although he shrugged off the mantle as much too smart for his home-ly shoulders, George Jessup was in many ways a fitting successor to William George Clarke.

Naturalist and historian W.G. Clarke, as he was invariably known, gave the region its name of Breckland in 1894. Such was his passion for the area he was reluctant to spend a night away from the warrens.

Clarke died in 1925, six years after George Jessup's introduction to Breckland's strange powers. When George died at eighty-eight, warm tributes pointed firmly to his devotion to 'this wild and lonely country'.

A resident of Watton all his years, George shared his Breckland enthusiasms in countless articles for local newspapers and magazines and with keenly supported illustrated talks. He often followed up with a coach tour of the area, adding a running commentary along the way.

Newcomers found him the perfect guide into fresh territories. Natives were often surprised to discover how little they knew about the countryside on their doorstep. Thousands of pounds raised for local charities gave George an extra glow of satisfaction.

He became hooked on Breckland before the Forestry Commission planted their armies of pine. Many other far-reaching changes, including the capture of several thousand acres for battle training, could not shake his faith in the old text: 'The heath admits few to its friendship, but it never falters in its choice.'

JIMMY NICHOLSON

Jimmy Nicholson enjoyed a larger ready-made audience than most when it came to stoking up Norfolk memories.

Weaned on steam, the colourful founder of Stalham Engineering Company could count on plenty of attention from his family – eight sons and six daughters for a start.

Indeed, all the lads joined the firm as it expanded and diversified, and they readily admit that father's passion for old engines fired and fed their specialised mechanical interests.

When Jimmy died at eighty-two, he left far more than a healthy engineering dynasty. Happily, he found time in later years to write, including best-selling autobiographical volumes *I Kept A'Troshin'* and *More Muck Than Money.*

> *The fire is getting low and the steam is going down. I have a boiler full of water so I shall soon pull the lever and put the hat on the chimney. I don't think I will bank the fire up tonight as I'm not going to trosh tomorrow.*

Those heartfelt lines stand as a fitting memorial to an outstanding Norfolk personality whose big family was matched by a wide circle of friends eager to glean knowledge and amusement from Jimmy's towering stack of stories.

Jimmy was only four when his grandfather introduced him to the threshing scene:

> *He travelled to work in a pony and cart and I used to ride wrapped up in a chaff bag. When we got to the engine I would sit there until he got the fire going. Then he would get me out and put me in the tender in the warm.*

Those tender mercies kept Jimmy going for many a year. His last threshing job came in 1967 as the combine harvester took centre stage.

TED BEALES

One of my prize possessions culled from over forty years in the local media is a letter about pail toilets.

It was sent to me by retired policeman Ted Beales from his Docking home in 1982, when the subject provided much enlightenment on the Radio Norfolk *Dinnertime Show.*

Ted was a prolific correspondent over the years, recalling countless amusing incidents from his time on the beat, and I also recall with gratitude how he stepped into the breach at a live broadcast from the

Sandringham Flower Show when a guest failed to appear. Ted was just warming up after a half-hour mardle.

He died at the age of ninety, and as a tribute – and after dining out on his story so often – I quote from that well-thumbed letter now turning yellow and curling at the edges:

> *A lad from a very rural part of Norfolk, whose lavatory was at the top of the garden, joined the Army. He was stationed at modern barracks and when he wrote his first letter home he stated: 'Dear Dad. This is the life! All mod cons, flush toylets etc, and when I cum hoom on leave I'll dew away wi' our ole petty at top o' the garden an' we'll hev a modern one.'*
>
> *The boy duly came home on leave, and on entering the garden gate he threw a hand grenade on to the small building which went up in a cloud of dust.*
>
> *At the same time his father opened the door and said: 'Yew shunt ha'done that, boy. Yar mother wuz in there.'*
>
> *When the old lady emerged from the rubble, covered in dust and pieces of brick and straw, the boy said most contritely: 'Oh, I'm ever so sorry, Mum.'*
>
> *She replied, as only a Norfolk mother could, 'That wunt yar fault, my boy. That must he'bin suffin I ett.'*

WINNIE CHAPMAN

Winnie Chapman was a character and a cook of the old school – my old grammar school at Swaffham. She served up delicious helpings of memories as we shared several reunions.

She died just short of her eight-sixth birthday after a long and happy retirement close to her loving family at Sporle. Winnie could match all my yarns from Hamond's as she reflected on her dinner-lady days before, during and after my Swaffham career.

She recalled keeping watch for boys who dared to go out of the school gate minus a cap, darning holes in the seats of their trousers after rough-and-tumble escapades, finding them a few coppers out of her own purse to spend at the tuck shop – and even chasing one of the masters with a dishcloth before discovering his true identity!

'I thought he was one of the boys, and he took it all in good part,' she smiled. That was Winnie's strength. She could always muster an extra slice of compassion when needed to go with the spotted dick and custard.

MAURICE TURNBULL

Maurice Turnbull was clerk to Mitford and Launditch Rural District Council when I started my local government reporting rounds in the early 1960s.

The council met at Dereham, village representatives employing various forms of transport to reach their destination.

On one memorable occasion an energetic local worthy arrived over an hour late, hands covered in grease and sweat dripping from his furrowed brow. 'Blasted puncture!' he bellowed by way of explanation.

'Don't worry. I'll organise a lift home after we have discussed these proposals for rural transport. Might even persuade the bus to go your way,' replied Maurice.

He died at eighty-one, a council official always ready to enlighten young reporters as he knew serious business ought to wear a broad smile.

ARTHUR AMIS

Arthur Amis was a proud Norfolkman who regarded his transition from cowman to political aide to two MPs as the work of 'a divine power'.

His passion for sharing knowledge and enthusiasms, including playing, watching and refereeing soccer, shone through so many crammed years centred on his home village of Trunch.

Arthur, who died at ninety-two, claimed the Norfolk Show 'clean milking' trophy outright after winning it five times in a row. He passed on his experience to Prince Philip at a Buckingham Palace garden party.

When the Prince talked of being taught about teats by Canadian dairymen, Arthur told him it was all wrong – and squeezed the royal finger from top to bottom to show him the proper way. A memorable Norfolk handshake.

They named a road after Arthur in Trunch while he was still alive, a tribute afforded to few while they are still about to appreciate it. A stalwart of the farm workers' union, agent for North Norfolk MPs Edwin Gooch and Bert Hazel and a Methodist local preacher for over sixty years, Arthur's humour, industry and sincerity made him an all round winner.

SIR MALCOLM BRADBURY

Sir Malcolm Bradbury was the most accessible of academics.

Perhaps my love of books made it easier to feel at home in the company of a literary genius, but his unfailing good humour and kindly manner made every meeting a delight.

During one radio interview when I let slip a bit more hyperbole than the subject demanded, he paid me the supreme compliment: 'My dear boy, you ought to start a school for creative talking...'

CHARLIE BOY SMITH

Charlie Boy Smith, whose colourful shirts matched his broad Norfolk repartee, bowed out in style.

One of the county's leading cultural ambassadors of recent times, he strummed and sang and laughed on a village hall stage just hours before he died at the age of seventy-eight.

Charlie needed no persuading to help warm up the audience with a few cheeky numbers at the Friends Of Norfolk Dialect's festive fling at North Elmham.

It turned out to be the final curtain on a long and fruitful career. I'm glad I was there to join in the applause for a Norfolk entertainer who gloried in his roots.

MOLLY CLAXTON

My great-aunt on the home front, Molly Claxton first saw Beeston light when the First World War was a year old.

She kept me and other village exiles in touch with our roots, a small but determined woman never soured by family ties and duties.

We gave thanks for her eighty-seven-year watch in the parish church on the hill surrounded by hedgeless fields and muddy lanes. Festive flowers lit up St Mary's as the Revd Jonathan Boston led an uplifting service on a dank afternoon.

'Your dad would have liked this pub,' I told him as we shared memories and refreshments afterwards in the Ploughshare.

Canon Noel Boston, round, rosy and genial during my Dereham reporting days, went a couple of rounds with Jem Mace, father of modern boxing and Beeston's most famous son, in an impromptu outstanding personality bout.

Mace's portrait looked down on us, a benevolent minder of the past as we caught up with current Beeston gossip about silly house prices, remaining characters and relations with neighbouring communities.

MICHAEL BRINDID

Michael Brindid was a carpenter who built his own platform from which to extol the virtues and delights of our precious dialect.

I got to know him well in recent years as he took to the stage for Cromer Festival dialect celebrations and Press Gang shows around the county.

He was a bit dubious about being introduced as 'the Chippendale of Hickling' even though I was at pains to stress it had more to do with his woodwork skills than his physical build.

Michael took it remarkably well when he was outshone by his wife Norah at the dialect festival deliberations. She collected the honours, but they turned it all to advantage in delightfully droll fashion with his monthly letter to the *EDP*.

GEOFFREY GOREHAM

Geoffrey Goreham was a teacher who never tired of passing on love and knowledge of his home city of Norwich.

As historian and author, Geoffrey could turn in a scholarly treatise on many aspects of city buildings and architecture.

But I reckon his most telling contribution to the debate came one orning as we exchanged a few parochial views about the thrum of constant traffic.

He invited me to take stock in and around St Stephen's. 'There – you could be just about anywhere in the country. Local names and local characters have been snuffed out in so many places, and now we look like joining them,' he sighed.

But that didn't stop him being optimistic and proud on his meandering rounds of the city he still loved.

SIR HARRY TUZO

General Sir Harry Tuzo was a soldier who fought to preserve the rural charms of his adopted county.

He was a formidable figure after such a distinguished Army record, most notably in Northern Ireland, but surprisingly easy to approach in his Norfolk retirement.

Our paths crossed regularly when he was president of the Norfolk Society, the county branch of the Council for the Protection of Rural England. He was in the audience when I gave a talk at Fakenham one evening and mustered sufficient daring to chastise him and his colleagues, albeit playfully, for being rather aloof.

I suggested Norfolk Society sounded elitist and it was time these custodians of the countryside came down from the mountain to embrace ordinary mortals.

'Will this do?' boomed the General as I stepped from the platform.

He threw a huge arm round my shoulder, shook a fearsome looking fist beneath my twitching nose – and then roared with laughter. We plotted the best strategy to keep Norfolk safe from the growing forces of greed and exploitation. 'A few more years and you'll be ready to join the elite,' was his parting shot.

JO AND GIMI JORDAN
Our friends have gone from the bottom of the loke but it will be some time before we stop peeking through their window.

His reading chair caught the best of the light. A passing tap and wave were regular interruptions he greeted with a wise old grin and 'Come in for a mardle if you have time' signal.

Her gentle pottering about in the kitchen area turned into a rapid response exercise as inevitable invitations to take tea, coffee or something stronger had been accepted. The headteacher still lurking within her ensured brisk organisation with a smile.

I often likened Jo and Gimi Jordan to a favourite great-aunt and uncle carrying a bottomless tin of sweets. Close neighbours dropped in to receive just as warm a welcome as that afforded friends from all over the world.

Their little Cromer home in Cross Street could resemble an impromptu United Nations meeting. Many's the time I was asked to bring a parochial edge to proceedings by 'torkin' Norfolk' to visitors from Holland, Italy, China and Cameroon.

We said farewell to Jo just before this wonderful partnership was due to celebrate a diamond wedding sparkle on Christmas Day.

Now Gimi has followed after a glorious sunset born from his belief that a day is wasted if you don't learn a new fact about life and writing.

In our early days at Cromer, the Skipper lads – fully alive to the hospitality and fun on offer – couldn't wait to rush down the loke to see 'Jimmyjo Jordan'. They made it sound like one person. They came to learn the meaning of inseparable.

We peek through the window out of habit. Empty chairs in a room full of voices and laughter. A tap and a wave and a tear of gratitude.

෴

5 Dewin' Diffrunt

There's a grain of eccentricity within us all. The trick is to let it ripen into the gloriously outlandish without trampling on every accepted standard of behaviour.

Perhaps the best eccentrics are those who amuse as much as amaze, fairly gentle souls who provoke a feeling of envy among their audience. 'Oh, I wish I had the courage to say something like that!' or 'How on earth does he get away with it?' are common coinage as a select few dispense their liberated largesse.

Good comedians can easily turn into bad judges of human nature through one insult too many, one profanity too far, so breaking the bond of affection and trust they had carefully nurtured.

Some eccentrics do drift towards the spotlight, but the majority of class acts stick to the 'real' world, blissfully unaware in many cases that they are offering an alternative to long-accepted conventions. 'If he knew he was an eccentric, he would stop being one' is a tantalising summary I stored away after a childhood meeting with a Norfolk gentleman of the road – 'a milestone inspector' said my father – as he passed through the village.

It never occurred to me to ask if choice or circumstance dictated his way of life. He was free, uninhibited and deserving of close attention. He quoted long passages from the Old Testament, specialising in Deuteronomy, wore a red rose in his buttonhole and acknowledged everyone he met. We admired rather than pitied as he marched on his colourful and cheerful way, probably to the next workhouse.

A few years ago I tried to interview Spike Milligan on the wireless. He had pushed eccentricity into an art form and made a lucrative living from it, although he admitted to suffering long periods of dark depression. His firecracker mind sparked *Goon Show* scripts into zany life. That must have been a wonderful experience, I enthused. 'NO!' he bellowed, 'it was sheer bloody murder! Sitting in a room trying to come up with funny lines week after week is no way to earn a living.'

That was one of two serious interludes in a broadcast of nearly an hour, including the bit where we normally had a news bulletin. The other came when I asked Spike if he liked being called a comedy legend. 'Boy, legends should be born out of death. I just want to be liked for making people laugh while I am alive.' Profound and rather humble.

So, with one of the finest examples of the age bearing his credentials, I am moved to usher onto the podium a few of my favourite home-made eccentrics. They took very seriously the old Norfolk dictum that 'dewin' diffrunt' is a highly commendable exercise.

Ralph Eustace Sherwin White was chief reporter on the *Yarmouth Mercury* during my stint with the weekly newspaper in the mid-1960s. He endeared himself, particularly to younger members of the staff who all called him Eustace, by regularly disappearing into a world of his own. This was most evident while he was composing his Scout column, a glorious mish-mash of anecdote, rumour, whimsy, fantasy and no-nonsense opinion, all tied up in extravagant similes by the yard.

We knew when a gem was coming. He'd rock back in his chair, clear his throat, exclaim loudly 'ah, yes!' with a self-satisfied smile and then transform his massive old typewriter into a machine gun spattering golden words all over the paper. Now and again we would be treated to an example of his creative powers – 'Britannia Pier sat in a sparkling sea like Neptune's frying pan waiting for a wash' – a little taster for the next big production.

Eustace occasionally forgot on which assignment he had embarked, usually dressed in blue beret, white mackintosh and brown sandals. His sou'wester and oilskin cape were reserved for wet days at any time of the year. We bumped into him one morning along busy Regent Road and inquired politely where he might be heading. 'I am down to cover Flegg Magistrates' Court,' he replied. We informed him that was next week, and, in any event, cases were heard in the Town Hall, completely in the opposite direction. He thanked us profusely, clicked his heels, turned sharply and expressed a fervent hope that he would arrive in time to cover the first case.

I also recall him searching frantically through the contents of a large dustbin outside the Halfway House pub in Gorleston, not far from his home. 'Give me a hand,' he called as I strolled past on my way to work. 'What are we looking for?' I asked, while crumpled packets, empty bottles, ripped magazines and an old pair of suede shoes mounted up beside me on a glorious May morning. 'I've lost a notebook,' retorted Eustace as if that were explanation enough. We didn't find it. He gave me a boiled sweet from rations kept deep in his coat pocket, returned all items to the dustbin and wondered if his wife could throw any light on the subject.

I worked alongside many colourful characters during my full-time years on newspapers and radio, but Eustace was a clear winner when it came to constantly idiosyncratic behaviour. This was prone to draw wide smiles rather than to set alarm bells ringing, although some of his predecessors in Norfolk didn't inspire unanimous gestures of benevolence.

Dr Messenger Monsey (1693–1788) never said anything commonplace and never did anything in a normal manner.

The son of a clergyman, he studied in Norwich and spent several years in private practice before being elected physician to the Royal Hospital at Chelsea. With appalling manners and vitriolic tongue, the Norfolk doctor was a novelty and an instant success in the capital.

He was reputed to be the only man who dared to contradict Sir Robert Walpole – Norfolk links clearly made him brave – and to beat him at billiards.

Monsey's party-piece was do-it-yourself dentistry. When one of his teeth ached he would tie it by a length of catgut to a perforated bullet and fire the bullet from a pistol. He claimed this method was painless and urged all his friends to try it.

When he went to the country, Monsey was in the habit of putting all his banknotes into the fireplace for safety, carefully hidden under kindling and coal. On one occasion he returned unexpectedly to find the housekeeper giving a tea party in his rooms, the fire blazing merrily.

His talk was vigorous and incessant, anecdotal, highly flavoured and crowded, like his torrents of letters, with classical quotations and deplorable puns.

His will was worthy of him. He insisted his body should be dissected and the remains thrown into the Thames. He left an old velvet coat to one friend and the buttons on it to another. A worthless snuff box was bequeathed to a certain young lady with 'lavish encomiums on her wit, taste and elegance'.

He took revenge on another lady by stating he would have left her a large legacy had he not discovered her to be a 'pert, conceited minx with as many affected silly airs as a foolish woman of quality'.

Louis John Tillett was senior partner of W.H. Tillett & Co., Solicitors, MP for Norwich, city councillor for the Mousehold ward – and an inveterate hater of trams.

While living at Catton during the early part of the twentieth century, he walked each day to his city office in St Andrew's, hitting every tram standard with his walking stick. On moving to Buxton, he took a taxi to the Whalebone public house and then resumed his striking progress on foot.

Tillett also objected to folk who gossiped on the pavement. He would take them firmly by the shoulders and transfer them to the gutter.

Even his funeral was an eccentric affair. There were no facilities in Norwich, so he was cremated in Ipswich. The coffin's final journey through Norwich was on a dray with no flowers or drapes.

James Webb became known as the Benevolent Stranger during the early-nineteenth century as he periodically doled out money to less fortunate members of the population.

On 2 February 1813 he called at the yard of the Angel Inn in Norwich, which stood where the entrance to the Royal Arcade is now found, in order to share his wealth with the masses. Word had spread and he was greeted by a large crowd of the idle and worthless.

Webb was forced to retire from the hostelry as a riot broke out, but not before he had distributed nearly £16 000. He moved on to another inn at Yarmouth, but had hardly started making donations to the waiting mob when noisy squabbling forced him to make another hurried departure.

Even so, before leaving the seaside for Bungay – where he was to hand out yet more money – he left in the care of a committee a large sum of cash to be shared among various Yarmouth charities.

Henry Lee Warner lived at Walsingham during the late-eighteenth century. He rose late in the evening, breakfasted at midnight and dined at around 4.30 in the morning. He invariably wore a gold laced hat, a waistcoat with deep slash worked sleeves and richly embossed buttons, and curved toed shoes with oblong buckles. He inherited the manors of Walsingham on the death of his father in 1760, but he was not cut out for management. His property deteriorated considerably within a few years.

Lee Warner's generosity knew no bounds, however, and his benign nature encouraged vandals and petty thieves to ravage and plunder his inheritance. Trespassers wandered unchallenged around the grounds surrounding his newly built manor of Walsingham Abbey, while the nearby plantation became a haven for local poachers. The worst an intruder could expect if confronted by Lee Warner was a mild ticking-off. Once, after catching an unwanted visitor clambering over a wall, he told him to take care how he got down for fear of hurting himself.

When the old squire died in 1804 at the age of eighty-two, the estates had fallen into such a bad condition it was estimated £20 000 would be needed to pay for repairs. Nevertheless, Lee Warner was buried in the local Abbey Church amid much pomp. One local newspaper's obituary column said he would be remembered not just for his idiosyncrasies but also for being a man 'in whom gentleman and scholar were happily blended.'

Margaret Fountaine was a Victorian woman who found amour among the butterflies. Her fascinating diaries remained in the storeroom of Norwich Castle Museum for nearly forty years.

She travelled unescorted to the most obscure and unwelcoming corners of the uncivilised world in search of butterfly specimens. Born at South Acre Rectory in 1862, Margaret led a conventional rural life until she became involved with a member of the Norwich Cathedral choir. They were almost engaged when he took his affections elsewhere. She sought solace in butterflies. She chased them through Italy by bicycle, she trekked through Hungary, travelling twelve hours a day and living on bread and sheep's milk.

Various men entered her life, but in Damascus a Syrian courier called Khalil Neimy won her heart. They roamed the world together for twenty-eight years. When he died she kept on roaming. Travels took her from North Africa, where she bathed in diluted creosote to keep off the leeches, and to the mountains of Tibet, riding a pony along precipitous tracks. 'Through a world of wild winds and bitter cold and strange, curious faces.'

Margaret Fountaine died on a dusty road in Trinidad in 1940, a butterfly net close by. Under the terms of her will, 10 mahogany display cases containing about 22 000 butterflies, her life's work, were delivered to the museum in Norwich. There was also a padlocked black box. This contained manuscripts, but could not be opened until 15 April 1978.

On that date the seals were broken and the lid lifted to reveal 12 identical volumes all filled with the neat handwriting of Miss Fountaine. They were her diaries from 1878, when she was not yet sixteen, until 1939, a few months before her death.

On top was a single sheet of paper: 'Before presenting this – the story of my life – to those, whoever they may be, one hundred years from the date on which it was first commenced…'

It spoke of 'the greatest passion of my life' and of Neimy, whose name the collection bore, and it ended, 'to the Reader, maybe yet unborn, I leave this record of the wild and fearless life of one of the South Acre children.'

Billy Bluelight, whose real name was William Cullum, has been afforded the rare accolade of having a Norwich pub named after him. He died in 1949 and a much-celebrated link with the old city was severed.

He made his name through running, mostly in races against the *Jenny Lind* steamboat. Starting from Foundry Bridge as she cast off, he set out at a jog-trot along the lanes and roads nearest the river, and would always be waiting on the bank at all the calling points to welcome the boat in and wave it out again.

Clad in shorts and singlet, with his usual imposing array of medals and gaily striped cricket cap, he made an interesting sight. His running prowess brought showers of coins at the end of his run, and these he would accept with an expansive smile and unshakeable dignity.

On the return journey he would boom out his little rhyme: 'My name is Billy Bluelight, my age is forty-five, I hope to get to Carrow Bridge before the boat arrive.' And he would be there. He remained 'forty-five' for years!

Other activities later in life enhanced his reputation as a Norwich character. He entered the commercial world as peddler of 'Mr Leach's cough remedy – good for coughs, colds and boys' chests'. His other notable enterprise was selling wild flowers at his favourite stand on the Walk at the Royal Arcade entrance. Colourful descriptions of his wares were highly individual. 'Primroses of natural growth and luxuriant foliage'. 'Nature's beauty' meant violets while 'Nature's natural flowers, penny a bunch' described his offering of daisies, marigolds and other wild flowers in season.

His dress was unconventional to say the least. Imagine a diminutive figure encased in a frock coat and resplendent in a top hat, wearing on his feet – white plimsolls. His eccentric appearance was further accentuated by innumerable medals plastered all over his chest. He was inordinately proud of these decorations, struck especially for him by friends to mark his feats of pedestrianism. He could proudly recount the history of each one.

It is not known how he got the name of Billy Bluelight, but that was how he was known to virtually all the citizens of Norwich between the 1880s and 1930s.

Harry Bensley made a rash boast over brandy and cigars in a London club – and it sent him on one of the most bizarre trails of the twentieth century.

The Thetford-born playboy overheard an argument between American millionaire John Pierrepoint Morgan and his English friend Lord Lonsdale over whether it might be possible for a man to walk around the world without being recognised. Bensley impulsively claimed it could be done. What's more, he would prove it.

Morgan took him up on the offer and bet Bensley $100,000 it couldn't be done, the equivalent of several million pounds in today's money. To make the challenge even more extreme, Morgan added several conditions.

Bensley would have to walk wearing an iron mask and pushing a pram all the way. He must find a wife on the journey, without removing the mask, and could take just one pound, a change of smalls and a supply of postcards for sale to fund his living expenses. At no stage could he identify himself, and a paid escort would ensure all conditions were fully met.

So, on New Year's Day, 1908, Bensley set off from Trafalgar Square to honour the bet, a trek that was to last six years, take him through 12 countries and bring 200 marriage proposals, all of which he claimed to have rejected.

Then as he reached Italy in 1914, the First World War broke out. The bet was off. The most popular explanation was that Bensley, a patriotic Englishman who had served in the Army in India as a young man, returned home because he wanted to fight for his country. Another version suggested Morgan cancelled the bet because he was worried the war would damage his steel empire.

Bensley did fight in the war but was invalided out after a year. His playboy lifestyle evaporated and he took on more mundane roles such as cinema doorman and YMCA warden. During the Second World War he was a bomb checker in an ammunition factory. He died, aged seventy-nine, in 1956.

Bensley's colourful legacy lives on in his home town of Thetford in the Ancient House Museum. Details of his barmy bet and some of the original postcards he sold are on permanent display. He is supposed to have sold a postcard to Edward VII for £5 when they met at Newmarket early on that memorable journey.

6 *Boyhood Daze*

It was good to discover I had a little in common with that great Irish writer, Seamus Heaney. My eyes fell eagerly on this heady recollection of farm life in Derry:

> *I spent time in the throat of an old willow tree at the end of the farmyard. It was a hollow tree with gnarled, spreading roots, a soft, perishing bark and a pithy inside. Its mouth was like the fat and solid opening in a horse's collar.*

Now, if he hadn't conjured such a wonder out of early days in Ireland, I would have moved in purposefully to claim it as one of the most telling snapshots from my Norfolk boyhood. I found a similar refuge only a few hundred yards from the old homestead ... but a thousand miles from boring errands, bossy grown-ups and gangland disagreements. My hiding place, my thinking corner, my safe house when village storms erupted, an old plastic sheet rescued from a nearby barn serving as makeshift roof for extra protection.

Of course, I created and shared a host of hide-outs with Tubby, Ernie and Rodney, some of them underground at the aerodrome and others tucked away down rutted tracks to nowhere. We swore secret oaths to defend each other and our current headquarters against all alien forces. We could vanish from the face of the Norfolk earth at a moment's notice. We scared ourselves with careless talk of coming under bombardment and not being able to escape before dark.

It was all part of a team effort which brought shape and purpose to long harvest holidays, a commitment to sticking together at work and play, sharing rewards and recriminations alike. But I kept the old hollow tree strictly to myself, and not just because it looked after my precious hoard of Woodbines and collection of songs snipped out of various music magazines. This is where I didn't want to be part of a group. I yearned for a solo career, to plough my own furrow, to pluck my own guitar, to revel in my own space.

I don't know if Seamus Heaney enjoyed a spit and a cough and then cleared his throat before branching out into a one-boy medley of hits from John McCormack and Josef Locke. If he did, I hope his willow-tree concert hall had better acoustics than mine. Earnest tributes to David Whitfield, Donald Peers and Dickie Valentine scarcely troubled any wildlife loitering around the roots of this countryside stage. If a breeze sprang up, it was easy to risk a burst or two of Lonnie Donegan and George Formby. A passing tractor would take it as no more than a small, harmless hedgerow creature protesting thinly at sudden disturbance.

There were silent sessions while I sulked, plotted, scribbled, prayed, seethed or just soaked up the peace. Time had no relevance in the old hollow tree. I nodded off more than once. I was always reluctant to leave its protective arms.

Part of the reason why my mates never suspected I had such a secret place rested with a long-held reputation for disliking trees. Well, I liked them to look at, as natural adornments all around our village world and for providing vital rations of apples, pears and walnuts. Two of them served as perfect goalposts on our orchard Wembley, while another made a useful wicket when we transferred the whole arena into Lord's. But a bad experience on Tubby's home patch involving the biggest Granny Smith apple provider left me desperately short of ambition to be any sort of social climber.

We were picking the best to sell from our roadside stall, and I was volunteered to go where no boy had gone before. Not too bad pushing skywards – but sheer calamity when I looked down. Tubby and the collecting pail were spinning out of control. I felt sick, dizzy and ready for a passing-out parade. I clung like a monkey to a wavering branch as it creaked menacingly. I started to cry, tears mixed with yells for someone to do something before I hurtled to certain oblivion and made cider of a few windfalls.

Tubby's dad took a breather from feeding the pigs to fetch a ladder and the best sympathetic mask he could muster. He was considerate enough not to inquire how I had reached such incredible heights on my own, and he patiently coaxed me down as Tubby worked overtime not to chortle. Tubby's mum, who had come to see what all the fuss was about, cheered me up with potted meat sandwiches, but I sensed a defining moment had been reached in my development as a rural adventurer.

The old hollow hideaway hardly qualified as a climbing challenge. Lolling nonchalantly over a mossy bank, it looked too casual, too familiar to hold any deep secrets. Easy to enter but hard to leave, I spotted it still shuffling over the landscape on a recent visit to my home village, a gnarled sentry keeping an ancient eye on my boyhood years.

I wanted to drop in, hum an old tune or two and curl up with a book of Seamus Heaney's poems. But I was frightened the rest of the gang might see me taking furtive steps into the past...

Funny Valentine

We tittered behind their backs, usually from the sort of distance reserved for unsociable dogs, flighty geese and grumpy bullocks. We flushed red in collective embarrassment whenever they caught us whispering in a furtive huddle. Most of the time we played safe and pretended they did not exist. Girls were hardly encouraged to point us towards that rickety rustic bridge from childhood to adolescence.

You had to sit next to them at village school. They had to put up with you for country dancing sessions. But when it came to organising revolutions and invasions, sorting out how to make two Woodbines last a whole week and planning where to locate the new gang headquarters, mawthers simply had no right to be anywhere near the action. The fact they wouldn't be seen dead within a mile of our plotting shed made no difference. This was Ladsville, 1950s style, and our regulations brooked no argument.

Then came the St Valentine's Day Massacre. Well, it was more of a minor skirmish, a gently skid along the muddy drift to growing up. Even so, it threatened to blow apart bonds of friendship holding together a quartet of inseparable adventure seekers. It wasn't the first crisis to confront us – memories of playground arguments over cigarette card collections and doctored conkers were still raw – but this carried certain ingredients never encountered before.

'Do you want to be married when you get older?' asked Ernie in a throwaway style that meant he had been giving the matter serious thought. The question was aimed at Tubby and Rodney as well, but they kindly side-stepped it until the silence became overwhelming and I felt obliged to say something to end the hiatus.

'Dunno ... that all depend ... she'd have to like cricket ... and *Educating Archie* ... and make proper dumplin's ... and not worry much if I was late home ...' I muttered and spluttered through an unconvincing list of female virtues plucked from nowhere, while my best chums chortled and tucked their thumbs behind braces to make them look older and wiser. Their scorn was tinged with pity, but that didn't make it any more bearable. They had set me up for a confession about the opposite sex, and I had fallen for it!

The follow-up was devastating. 'We hear you'll be sending a Valentine's card this year. Thass nice to be soppy, but we can't be smooth like you.'

It sounded more like a sneer than a compliment. I turned crimson with rage and discomfort, not least because I had no idea who they were referring to. Yes, there had been a note at milk time only a few weeks earlier to a girl whose brother had a *Roy Rogers Annual* he was prepared to lend out. I did get a fly in the eye while cavorting in the sun last summer and appeared to be crying near the railings when Maisie Bennett produced her initialled hankie for emergency use. Those kind of episodes could spark fanciful rumours, but I had done nothing to encourage them. Honest.

Ernie continued to relish the role of romantic raconteur. 'Whole point of Valentine's is you don't have to say who they're from. My Dad tell me he used to tie a parcel to a long bit o'string, knock on the door, hide up round the corner and then pull the parcel away when this girl came to see what was there. So she dint get noffin ... and she dint even know who wuz snatchin' onnit back!'

He roared at the homely picture. Tubby and Rodney joined in. I remained angry and wanted to dismiss it as a puerile exercise totally out of keeping with the spirit of February 14th. Not that I knew anything about such strange antics surrounding this date...

'Who am I supposed to be sending a card to?' I inquired with as much mystery and gravity as I could muster.

'Well, if you don't know, that make it even more fun,' suggested Tubby, whose own overtures in this area had been mainly confined to insulting his older sister. 'I'll tell your beloved thass from someone else,' volunteered Rodney with an exaggerated wink and a knowing smile that belied his widespread ignorance on this subject and all other cherished traditions.

I could tell my serious probing would prompt nothing but more teasing and evasion, so I decided to go on the attack and warn my smirking colleagues against breaking our brotherhood's sacred code of honour. This embraced clear rules on supporting each other at all times and especially in the face of formidable female wiles, summarised succinctly in two words – 'No girls!' There could be no relaxing our guard over silly Valentine messages, coded or otherwise. We had to stand firm, together, unflinching, defiant. They took the point made passionately from my straw-bale hustings. A fresh surge of comradeship throbbed through our renewal of vows. They confessed to making it up about me and the Valentine's card. Then Ernie made full recompense for leading this unprovoked assault on my pride and sensibilities. At his behest we agreed to send each other two Valentine's apiece, crammed with sentimental couplets and 'Guess Who?' lines dripping with undying affection.

Boys outside our tight little circle were jealous. Girls beyond our world altogether were utterly confused. We flaunted our cards at playtime, wondering noisily who on earth could be smitten so deeply by our rough-and-ready charms.

Dairy disaster

My abject failure to rise to the top as a dairy worker was all the more pointed because of a proud family tradition. Dad and my two older brothers were expert stockmen, each entrusted with full milking duties long before I heard the call to lend a hand.

Despite the cosy-sounding names like Buttercup, Clara and Strawberry, cows with swollen udders always seemed too frisky, too impatient, for my liking as they trooped into the parlour. Yes, they were prepared to stand and deliver twice a day, every day of the year, but good yields depended on as little messing-about as possible and provision of as much good food as could be scoffed in the time allotted.

A short-lived but dramatic career as a milking-time operative started with the role of food preparer, turning chaff and root cutters with all the speed and energy my little arms could muster. Mangolds, turnips and swedes surrendered their sweet juices to my mixture of sweat, grunts and groans. As the handle slowed, demands for extra chopped supplies increased. Cows' heads were lost in mangers and shadows as I struggled in with another brimming skep. Manners were appalling when I ventured close enough to realise these animals would eat me as well if I got jammed up against the whitewashed wall.

Next stop along the milky way was being put in charge of the cooler, a simple but fascinating device which could mesmerise young boys into complete lethargy on a balmy summer's evening. A hose was connected to the pipe at the side of the radiator-like contraption and cold water passed through the metal coils and out through a pipe at the bottom. Milk from a drum container at the top was then allowed to pass over the crinkles, collecting in the trough at the bottom and flowing down finally into the big churn.

My trough overflowed a few times because I forgot to release milk for the churn underneath, an oversight that curdled my new nickname of 'Halfpint' into something far less flattering. When I overlooked to notice that the churn underneath was full, well, the language was enough to make Buttercup and Clara blush ... as soon as they'd finished chomping.

Things really hotted up when I left the cooler and its crinkled delights and graduated to a top post at the very heart of the milking operation on Primrose Farm. Brother Malcolm elevated me to the cream of dairy society because the boss was on holiday and no one else was available to help. My incentive to do well was the promise of a proper milker's hat with the peak at the back, a promise never fulfilled but often mentioned in dispatches about my cowshed calamity. I heard it suggested more than once that such fancy headgear perfectly suited a brain slipping loose from its moorings.

These cows did their best to help on my big debut, marching swiftly to their own regular stalls and waiting for halters to be fixed. Steaming flanks gave them an eerie, ghost-like quality as I made them secure, washed teats, attached suction cups and listened for the hungry slurp of machines doing their jobs. A nod of approval from big brother as the rhythm built and the ritual unfolded yet again. He urged me to chat to my charges, relaxing them for full production along with a friendly slap or nuzzle. It seemed I had arrived as a useful recruit to the village milking army. Sad to say, I was wearing a demob suit of sackcloth and ashes before the evening was out.

Perhaps I relaxed more than the cows, sheer pleasure at managing to get through initial tests giving way to a dangerous brand of bravado. Maybe I should have noticed the glint in Mirabelle's eye as she turned her head, chewed contentedly and just checked it was the new boy fussing and chuntering behind. In any event, my complacency was shattered as I went to set her free from the stall. She turned to leave with a hearty swish of the tail – and I realised with horror that I had forgotten to separate her from the milking machine.

I cannot recall the exact sequence of events, but there was clanging against concrete fairly early on and a stomach-churning sound of lovely fresh milk racing along the gutter into the drain somewhere near the end. I panicked throughout, cursing Mirabelle, machinery and the whole milking maelstrom. Big brother had a few choice words for me before he caught up with the overloaded cow and restored a bit of order.

Production was a few gallons down that evening, but nowhere as low as my self-esteem. I had blown the big chance. Tears welled up to cast doubt over that old adage about not crying over spilt milk. I was banished to the cutting and grinding arena for the rest of the week, preparing giant salads for beasts I knew were mocking me while they faced the other way.

I often chew the cud over that dairy disaster and wonder if I would have fared any better in the butter and cheese department. Can't think why, but they never put me forward for the entrance exam.

Taken to book

I admit to nursing a bit of a work-shy streak in my formative years, especially when the nights started pulling in and countless ripping yarns called out for attention up a quiet corner. 'You'll never have so much time again to read for pleasure,' I told myself, nudging aside requests to clean shoes, chop sticks and contribute on a more regular basis to the general wellbeing of a large family in a small country cottage.

My reasoning was that there were so many others able and willing to carry out mundane tasks, it mattered not if I skulked out of the way while they were being sorted. Should this logic fail and my page-poring presence be seriously disturbed, there was always the dastardly ploy of carrying out certain chores in such a ham-fisted, hopeless manner that return invitations were highly unlikely. A dangerous strategy at times – I risked instant eviction one night by sticking to my fireside chair when a dramatic fall of soot down the chimney threatened to turn me into an Al Jolson look-alike – but at least they all knew where I stood when it came to the common cause. Or, to be more accurate, where I sat ... with my nose in a book.

Eventually, with grammar school demands growing alongside my reputation for knowing that Kipling did more than make cakes and Shakespeare was not born at Stratton Strawless, I exchanged the guise of domestic sluggard for budding eccentric. Family smiles said it all when we had visitors. 'He'd rather sit and read than help about the place, bless 'im, but at least we know where he is on dark nights.' Most of father's colleagues on the farm sighed little sighs of regret at the imminent snipping of a traditional strand. Then they brightened considerably at the prospect of Norfolk agriculture being allowed to carry on without any long-term intervention from me.

Perhaps the only occasion on which I felt a twinge of guilt came when a village elder I liked and respected upbraided me for 'wearstin' orl that time book-larnin''. This verdict may have been coloured by my refusal to put down George Orwell's *Coming Up For Air* in favour of a couple of hours on his garden where the plot thickened with unkempt vegetation. Even so, I was stung sufficiently to ask him what he meant by 'wasting time'. He saw my hurt, softened immediately and reduced the indictment to 'missin' harf woss a'gorn on while yew're got yar snout in a book'. I pleaded guilty, and asked for a few other chapters to be taken into consideration while he looked for a more suitable gardener.

Ironically, I soon felt obliged to defend my rural friends and relations against constant accusations from more 'sophisticated' town and city dwellers about blatant time-wasting in the sticks. With the sort of superior sneer that can hide a hint of envy, they pointed to an inordinate amount of dawdling and gossiping in and around country lanes as a perfect guide to profligate behaviour.

Look how a quick trip to the farm for a pint of milk turned into a tea-drinking marathon with an acre-by-acre dissertation thrown in for good measure. Or the way a call at the shop for a bar of soap or tin of treacle was transformed into something like an old-tyme music hall, with banter and bonhomie flowing freely either side of the counter. And what about 'passing the time of day' with all and sundry rather than moving on swiftly to the next job and destination?

I winced at such soulless chuntering. Oh, a thousand apologies for not clocking-on and clocking-off at the behest of a hooter, but the countryman tends to work when there is work to do and rest when there isn't.

Sorry for the quirky style, but there is an inclination in these uncivilised parts to measure time in a slow succession of seasons, a rotation of crops underlining the natural process of growth and decay, then growth again.

We humbly beg your pardon, but the odd moment must be found to stand back from the tumult of modern life to watch the autumn shadows grow, to listen to the small music of hens or soughing in the old walnut tree.

Yes, we're a very strange lot. But all that mardling, mooching and musing has nothing on Friday- night bathtime in front of the kitchen fire. You should see me whooshing myself through the water, a wave rising up behind big enough to swamp the mat and endanger the very fire itself with the sudden flood.

I may have laid it on a bit thick when They accused Us of needing missionaries and time-and-motion experts. Still, it seemed a reasonable means of showing the true value of having your nose in a book when boring jobs were being handed out. I have always preferred imagination to perspiration.

Real horse power

With a couple of gentle giants still nodding their way through all seasons on the farm where my father worked, and a riding school at full canter just up the road, I accepted horses as an integral part of my boyhood world.

Even as full-scale mechanisation revved up on the headlands and our pretty, twisty lanes waited for a trickle of traffic to turn into a roaring torrent, our four-legged friends whinnied and snorted at such mundane progress. I sensed their defiance might carry more than a nosebag of nostalgia, although limited experience told me to maintain a respectful distance.

My first harvest adventure saw me tossed like a small wheatsheaf onto Snowball's back for a dramatic finale, a triumphant trek to the stack with the last load of summer. I clung on for dear life, frightened of banging my head against the clouds or making an ignominious slide into the pointed stubble. Bigger boys and seasoned men chuckled at my discomfort before they formed a human ladder to deliver me safely back to earth. I have shied away from heights ever since.

A short but colourful career as a 'howd gee' boy suited my low-level temperament much better, leading the horse as a harvest wagon trembled with sheaves, and yelling a warning to men balanced precariously on top to hold tight. Sadly, the art of doing two things at once regularly proved beyond me and there were times when a lofty hideaway would have been useful as protection against retribution at refreshment time.

Another telling experience in my equine education is worth trotting out to help explain a general reluctance to find these creatures endearing. Billy Ketteringham, son of Florrie, our amiable and patient next-door neighbour, did most of his travelling by pony and trap. Whenever he tethered up our way I kept on about being taken for a ride and asking Tiny to 'gee up' past the orchard and into the heart of the village. Billy relented one day and I sat proudly beside him as we clip-clopped into the limelight. I pulled a blanket over my knees, just like the grown-ups did, made clicking noises to inspire the little black pony to go quicker and waved regally to all we passed. I was left in charge while Billy made a 'quick call' at the Ploughshare pub, gripping the reins and imploring Tiny not to make too many marks on the shingle yard when he shuffled impatiently.

Evidently, Billy met an old friend from the dealing circuit. They owed each other a drink. As they exchanged pleasantries in the bar, my anxiety grew alongside Tiny's appetite for renewed action. I felt control slipping away and so stood up on the seat of the trap, my knuckles whitening under the strain of pulling at the reins, and shrieked for help. Billy emerged just in time to save me from auditioning for a part in Ben Hur's chariot race. I never pestered for a ride again.

Of course, we turned ourselves into willing riders of the most fleet-footed animals going in the school playground, especially after cheering through another epic western at the village hall picture show. A smart smack of the backside, excited cries of 'giddyup!' and 'race you to the sheriff's office' and we went full gallop through Hopalong Cassidy's latest routine. Only those with the true gift of synchronisation attempted impersonation of Roy Rogers or Gene Autry strumming and singing as they cantered along the cactus-packed trail.

When we were deemed bright enough to make comparisons between what had been and what was replacing it, older workers on the farms around us pointed to the special relationship enjoyed by man and horse as they struggled together through all weathers. Horses were the most important creatures in East Anglia up to the last war. 'Good horses, good farm' is a saying that rang so true across the acres. The men looked after the horses as well as worked with them, and took great pride in the appearance and standard of their teams. There was keen competition among the farms – braid and ribbons, shining coats and harness in perfect condition. For all my misgivings about going anywhere near the saddle, I could understand why rosettes were handed out to mark that proud partnership.

The transition from one kind of horse power to another wasn't without its traumas. We heard about Arthur, a horseman of long-standing, being instructed in the art of using the new blue Fordson Major tractor and the powerlift furrow plough. He stalled the engine in the middle of the field on his maiden voyage. Arthur dismounted and gave a quick pull on the starting handle. The tractor was still hot and still in gear. It started up immediately and began to buck in alarming fashion.

Arthur jumped back, waved his cap and kept on shouting, 'Whoa, yer beggar! Whoa, yer beggar – whoa!'

Old habits die hard. Perhaps it is just as well that I steered clear of them before Snowball and Tiny claimed me as a stable companion.

Fête worse than...

The village fête remains one of the highlights on the social calendar, even though it can betray weaknesses as well as advertise strengths. Those who work overtime to put up stalls, sell tickets and organise competitions could easily feel a kind of superiority over fellow-parishioners they haven't seen since last summer. A bit like the local shopkeeper who becomes popular all of a sudden in winter when snowdrifts block the roads.

Still, the truly committed few have always been ready with defiant industry to mock the old chorus of 'people don't muck in like they used to.' While the rural dream may be threatened by the ever-encroaching urban nightmare in some areas, faithful little flocks will persist in decking out their acres with traditional values.

Bowling for the pig, guessing the weight of the cake, how many sweets in the jar or the name of the home-made doll, throwing darts, tossing hoops, turning cards, spinning wheels, poking straws, rolling pennies ... how we loved those old favourites trotted out on the meadow near the aerodrome, while Guy Mitchell's latest hit bounced across the runway. Postwar austerity got lost in a lather of reckless spending under a relentless June sun, and fun and frolics continued as perfect partners at the dance after tea in the Nissen hut that served as our village hall. Fête day was the longest day of the year for community spirit to flow.

Pillow fights on the greasy pole carried obvious hazards, but it became apparent that the most dangerous item on the fête scene was the fancy dress competition. Dutiful vicars and their wives seemed to shoulder much of the social burden, although a parish near ours hit on a bright idea to draw potential sting from this eagerly awaited parade. 'We ask someone famous they don't know to do the judging, and that can save a lot of bother,' smiled a veteran, clearly delighted at this celebrity-based breakthrough after years of fears about civil war replacing forced smiles, polite applause, knowing glances and dark mumbles.

My Coronation Year furlong as a jockey aside, I resisted calls to the dressing-up arena, contenting myself instead with the role of ringside reporter as Ernie, Rodney and Tubby asked for a running commentary. I didn't realise how valuable these observations would prove many summers later when invitations came to open fêtes – 'and would you be good enough to judge the fancy dress for us?'

I had seen local luminaries with several relatives and countless friends on display cajoled into service. If they made once choice they stood accused of favouritism, and if they made another choice there was every chance of being cut off in certain wills or being shunned completely when the posh Sunday tea invitations went out.

I had watched MPs or would-be Members run the risk of losing votes as mothers scowled their disapproval, aunties informed them that they'd stayed up half the night putting that lot together and big brothers swore to avenge a tear-stained youngster.

I accepted all these dangers and tried to minimise them by placing them up in lights before a mark was awarded in anger – 'We only have so many prizes, so some of you are going to be disappointed … I think you all look wonderful, but I have the really tough job of making a final decision … I'm sure mums can explain to their children why it's good to take part even if you don't get a prize … and I'm sure children can explain to mums why it's good to take part even if you don't get a prize…' Choppy waters, but you have to pretend you have the proper oars before pushing the prize boat out.

Even so, it is still hard to decide how one Crocodile Dundee is a more snappy dresser than his cork-dangling shadow, or how the small pillar-box carries a bigger stamp of authenticity than the other one with more sensible collecting times. If there are four contestants but only three prizes, it may be worth declaring a dead heat for third place and leaving the organisers to come up with the goods. They have to live there without encouraging civil war. They'll come up with the goods.

One school of thought tells you warm applause and unanimous acceptance can automatically follow selection of the smallest or the youngest or the cutest competitor as the main prizewinner. Perhaps that is the soft option. Old hands with a hard streak can peer beyond chubby pink cheeks and dewy blue eyes. I find it impossible.

But I can resist the urge to bounce babies in a row and categorise them into 'bonny', 'beautiful' and 'she eats all her rusks and sleeps like a top every night'. I dread the thought of some nipper placed out of the top three growing up with an unquenchable thirst for retribution, haunting me, haranguing me as I try to guess the name of the cuddly teddy bear.

Perhaps we judges should be grateful that the carnival queen and her attendants have been chosen before the big day. Just imagine that little task being added to all others in front of an expectant audience. Could be a fête worse than death if you made an unpopular selection.

Harvest home

Glinting stubble formed an obvious runway from summer into autumn. How we cheered final loads wobbling from each field and stared in fresh admiration as Charlie Powley underlined his reputation as a thatcher supreme. There he goes, biking home for tea with his handiwork emerging like a strawed temple behind him. Harvest's crowning glory in the setting sun.

Shack-time meant a feast for poultry turned out on shorn acres to snaffle up any remaining grain. Harvest home meant riots of glorious colours and scents in decked-out Chapel and Church, and the communal supper with home-made entertainment to celebrate completion of another coronation of the year. The age-old ritual involved nearly everyone in the village, so thanks were loud and sincere.

We knew this time of the year was the signal for men on the farm to start muttering about 'nights soon pullin' in' and 'gittin' late earlier'. But rousing harvest hymns threw a protective cloak over headlands and hedgerows where spiteful little winds were waiting to usher in a colder, darker season. We took liberties with some of the most familiar lines as my mother and Bertha Naylor took it in turns to accompany the Chapel's most fervent singing of the year:

> *All is safely gathered in,*
> *Some's bin troshed and sent to Lynn...*

This was our afternoon variation. A bit more bravado kept pace with the wheezing organ during the evening service, although we took care to sit near the back and not giggle with guilt as a new version crept over the pews:

All is safely gathered in,
'Cept George King's, he's late agin…

Flowers hid the pulpit. A harvest loaf in the shape of a sheaf shone like gold at the heart of so much produce, the bulk of it gleaned from flourishing local gardens, orchards and kitchens. One boy kept nudging and pointing to six rosy apples balanced neatly on an enamel plate beneath the board displaying hymn numbers. He had handed over the fruit at Sunday School that morning with an earnest plea: 'Here's half a dozen apples for the harvest sale; can you thank mother for twelve?' Well, it was quite a lengthy walk with his mates, and all that fresh air could work up quite an appetite.

The sale of produce the Tuesday after was one of the social highlights on our village calendar. You could find out who was top of the crops when it came to scrubbed potatoes, creamy parsnips, handsome onions and rust-proof beans. 'What am I bid for this bag of King Edward spuds?' 'Half-a-crown if they come from Reggie Bennett's garden!'

A jar of Mrs Symonds' home-made raspberry jam fetched more than anyone else's. Mrs Bird's bottled fruit and Mrs Dack's brown eggs left others in the shade. Mrs Burrell's sponges were still the lightest. It developed into something like an unofficial parish competition, good-natured and highly lucrative under the homely stewardship of Harry Dawson. He had a good word for everyone. Everyone liked him. Our annual harvest auction simply reaffirmed the respect and affection in which he was held both inside and outside his beloved Methodist Chapel.

The harvest supper, or horkey as the elders insisted on calling it, was primarily a Church affair, held in the Rectory Room. But there was no block on Chapel folk who wanted to join the parson's flock congregated either side of trestle tables groaning with goodness. A traditional toast acted as an eagerly awaited starting pistol:

Here's health to our master
The lord of the feast;
God bless his endeavours
And send him increase.

Older boys and girls who had helped with the crop gathering were deemed worldly enough to hear country tales, some carrying an earthy edge, and to savour a modest sip or two from the jug of ale doing regular rounds. My first taste of beer in public at a harvest supper remains a potent milestone on the rural road to social acceptability. Frankly, I didn't go much on the beer, but I relished the way everyone looked at me while I was drinking.

'Give us a song, boy!' found me ready with a medley of current favourites, including 'I Remember the Cornfields', 'My Truly', 'Truly Fair', 'The Shrimp Boats Are Coming' and 'My September Love'. The big-ballad finish sparked loud applause and eager offers of more grown-up refreshment:

> *And in December*
> *Still glows the ember*
> *Of my September love.*

It takes a useful performer to swear undying love to maidens yet to be met, but I knew now I'd be set fair for any romantic challenges across the golden stubble of time.

◎◎

7 Village Byways

It may not add up to very much in the Great Scheme of Things, but I derived immense pleasure from a Norfolk double on our family half-term rounds.

We allowed our imaginations full paddle in countless creeks on a coastal run which began under listless skies and ended in a fiery-orange sunset.

We squeezed down the narrowest of lanes for a few inland diversions dotted with churches, surrounded by history and snow-drops, and invitations to explore deeper when hedges grow heavier with secrets.

Then came the Creakes, like brazen brothers determined to be noticed at a genteel family reunion ... well, that's how they struck me after so much meandering and musing in forsaken byways around them.

Perhaps my thoughts were coloured by two lads growing a mite restless in the back of the car. I knew how to impress them, spelling it out before we resumed our coastal route.

'There we are – you have been knee-deep in creeks and Creakes today. Did you know South Creake used to have a brewery, a razor blade business and was home to Farmer's Glory breakfast cereal?'

I pointed out a complex of buildings with a tall tower on the main street, main clue to a past full of industry and innovation. Nods of interest, but it was easier to claim genuine attentions and conjure pic-tures in and around those other creeks.

Thornham harbour provided the perfect berth for a picnic before careful inspection of barnacled and broken ribs in a haunting coastal graveyard.

Wind, sky, water, mud, boats, sparse grass, swooping birds, muffled trippers ... the scene deserved its sunny tint as emotions were towed beyond the usual markers.

Wells was rubbing winter sleep from its eyes. Morston and Blakeney were alive, alive O with signs advertising mussels for sale. Stiffkey wore a satisfied little smile as traffic had no option but to creep quietly through its tight and twisting centre.

Time, pace and seasons mattered little as we settled for a glimpse of the sky-wide fields along the dyke at Burnham Overy Staithe. This is the spiritual heartland of poet, Anglo-Saxon scholar and children's writer Kevin Crossley-Holland.

As we sat and looked and felt, I recalled lines from his poem, 'Here, at the Tide's Turning':

> *This year, next year, you cannot think*
> *Of not returning; not to perch in the blue*
> *Hour of this blunt jetty, not to wait, as of right,*
> *For the iron hour and the turning of the tide.*

We'll be back, seeking new from the old. And we know this part of Norfolk never disappoints.

Tranquil waters

The invitation to embark on a voyage of discovery in little Themelthorpe's tranquil waters came from Edna Buckley on her eighty-eighth birthday.

She sent me a card with an offer hard to refuse from her rural retreat snuggling between Reepham and Foulsham.

As long as I promised to be quiet and well behaved, I was welcome to stroll round the wonderful gardens at Wood Farm ... with raspberries and cream to follow for Sunday tea.

It seemed the ideal way to find out more about this community of 65 souls. My wife and lads could tell I was rather excited as we advanced into deepest Norfolk, and so pointed firmly to Edna's warning about conduct.

The setting was idyllic and there were strolling players on parade from various parts of the county by the time we spotted signs and bunting. Clearly the twelfth-century church of St Andrew's nearby was in for a good afternoon, and so it proved, with more than £1000 raised towards its upkeep.

Brian and Pat Norbury started the inspired transformation around Wood Farm in 1964. At that time there were just four substantial trees.

The rest was a wilderness. Although most of the names on our botanical list left me floundering amid the herbaceous borders, water lilies, shrubberies and woodland walks, I tried to nod approval at the right times as compliments flowed.

We took tea under the trees, and then it was time to seek out Edna to thank her and her Themelthorpe friends for this family treat. 'Good of you to come!' beamed the mother-figure as she organised introductions.

I discovered she was originally a Reymerston mawther and that Jack Juby, one of the county's leading personalities in the horse world, was her brother.

Then came a splendid bonus in the shape of a big black folder holding a comprehensive project on Themelthorpe prepared at school by the Norbury's son Graham. The fact it was twenty years old detracted little from its role as the perfect village commentator.

After all, two decades in a spot like this have much more to do with unbroken charm than with unbridled change.

A new house spells dramatic development, a new face demands full-scale inspection.

Here are just a few snippets about Themelthorpe from Graham Norbury's project:

- *Spelling of the village has long given trouble. Old documents include the variations Thimblethorpe and Tymbelthorpe. A letter arrived a few years ago addressed to The Melthorpes!*
- *Themelthorpe Common was enclosed in 1811. In fact, most of the common was in the parish of Foulsham.*
- *St Andrew's Church has only ever had one bell. It was repaired and rehung in 1996. The church once had a thatched roof.*
- *The Methodist chapel, built in the 1880s, closed in 1978. Rebecca Yarham brought Methodism to the village in the early nineteenth century, and the first congregations met in a farm kitchen.*
- *Between 1920 and 1934 the village became a hive of activity for one day every April. All work stopped and everyone went to watch steeple chasing on a meadow off Dicky Lane.*
- *In July, 1943, Edith Claxton travelled from Themelthorpe to Buckingham Palace to receive a bravery award. A member of the Red Cross and a senior Civil Defence warden, she gave first aid to a seriously injured soldier after a mine exploded in the area.*
- *The village pub, the Fox and Hound, closed in the 1920s and is now a private home called Foxen House.*

Enticing corners

Strange how life turns round.

That little thought struck me forcefully during the spell when an unrelenting sun beat down on Norfolk.

When I was a lad among harvest fields in the middle of the county, our annual trip to the seaside stood out as the biggest treat of the year.

Now I live on the coast. If it gets too hectic for comfort, I head inland for a spot of refreshments and reflection in rural pastures.

We are well blessed in North Norfolk with so many enticing corners to soothe the fevered brow. Just a couple of minutes and a couple of miles from one world to another. From bustle to balm.

A picnic in the grounds of Felbrigg Hall demands a good walk for afters; round by the lake and on through the fields to St Margaret's Church, which still comes as a delightful surprise no matter how often you call.

At one time the village of Felbrigg surrounded the church. Now this medieval building, with its memorial to historian Robert Wyndham Ketton-Cremer, who left the hall to the National Trust, has the place to itself amid rolling acres.

Another day, another stately home, another picnic. We found shade next door to the glorious ruins of another church dedicated to St Margaret, this one a short distance from Wolterton Hall. And yes, this was where the old village used to be.

The ancient tower seemed to glance down approvingly as we strolled with history. A long brick wall held back the rest of the world as we followed a path leading into cooling woods and out again into piercing sunshine.

The parkland lake dazzled. Sheep could scarcely muster an inquisitive look. By the time we reached the old horse pond, other visitors were preparing for Wolterton Hall's last conducted tour of the day.

Langham is far enough away from the holiday beat to have a mind of its own. Neat and welcoming, it appears to be in constant readiness for a visit from the Best Kept Village judges.

We enjoyed a meal and a mardle at the Bluebell, a pub at the heart of the community and therefore able to maintain its character through major refurbishment. A short stroll to the churchyard to pay respects to a man of the sea who retired here to farm and write. (Did he inspire Henry Williamson a century later?)

Captain Frederick Marryat, whose seven novels belonging to the Langham period included *Children of the New Forest*, died in 1848 and is buried in the churchyard. He had four sons and seven daughters. Only one son, Frank, survived him – and he died at the age of twenty-eight.

From tomb to dome. There it squats on the edge of the old Langham airfield like an upturned Norfolk dumpling. It was an anti-aircraft training dome, probably the only one to go up in Norfolk.

Puckish thoughts about millennium madness started to surface as the sun went down. Home to Cromer. It had stopped heaving, the air was fresh and I needed to make sure the pier was still there.

Nautical touch

Family meanderings developed a strong nautical theme – and not just because our village trail ran close to the coast.

Our half-term safari began with a picnic on the grassy patch outside Nelson's church at Burnham Thorpe. Scaffolding around the tower signalled the start of a restoration programme.

A constant delight of visits to this church and this Burnham is to note the way Norfolk's most famous son is celebrated with quiet pride rather than crass commercialism.

Brancaster Staithe village hall was our next port of call to size up Ken Tidd's latest exhibition. The bait-digger-turned-artist continues to make wonderful use of the watery world around him.

More rain threatened as we reached Heacham, land of the lavender fields and Princess Pocahontas. She married local lad John Rolfe in 1614, and brought peace between settlers in Virginia and the indigenous Native Americans.

She appears on Heacham's village sign, and there's a memorial in the parish church 'to mark a picturesque episode in the history of two nations'. Pocahontas is buried in Gravesend, where she died of consumption at twenty-two, while her husband's grave is in Virginia.

'Have you seen the oval plaque above the door?' asked a regular member of the Heacham congregation who recognised me from a recent appearance with the Press Gang at Sedgeford village hall.

The plaque lists 12 Heacham people:

... who went in a boat from the shore on a party of pleasure, and were unfortunately drowned on Sunday, the second day of June, 1799.
'This monument was erected by dear friends and neighbours not only as a testimony of regard and lively sorrow for their much

lamented fate; but also as a memorial to warn the rising and future
generations against rashly engaging in similar undertakings, lest
they be brought to the same untimely end.

Heacham played an important role in the early history of trade union-
ism. On 5 November 1795, over 200 poor farmers and day labourers
met in the parish church to organise their claims for a reasonable wage.
The attempt failed as a result of anti-sedition laws introduced that
same month.

The Heacham attempt at organised labour came thirty-nine years
before the Tolpuddle Martyrs. That could be worth remembering if
they hold a pub quiz at the King William IV in nearby Sedgeford.

So there's much more to Heacham than lavender and Pocahontas.

Sensitive growth

During fantasy-fed minutes away from the usual track of life I vote
myself a member of Norfolk County Council's planning committee.
My first job is to oversee the growth of this splendid county in a sensitive
but forthright manner during another decade of challenge and change.

To cope with the continued influx, and to safeguard wishes of the
indigenous remnants at the same time, I propose a policy of using
existing communities to absorb the extra population instead of allowing new villages and towns to be built.

For example, this means Smallburgh grows into Large-burgh,
Mileham turns into Seven Kilometres, Scole is upgraded to
University, Hindringham become Helpful, Seething is transformed
into Cheerful, and Melton Constable takes on the role of Norfolk CID
headquarters.

You get the idea, and might well be inspired to give your own village or town a useful makeover, especially if you live in Baconsthorpe,
Winfarthing or Burston. (Extension to the Rhine, decimalisation and
building a new public toilet spring to mind.)

There are Norfolk settlements, however, where growth – or change
of any marked kind – would be sacrilege. I called on one such place
the other evening, glorying in its comparative isolation off the busy
Holt–Fakenham road.

Trying hard to snuff out impish thoughts about dormitories and
insomniacs, I turned left at Little Snoring and followed the lane to
much-smaller Kettlestone.

It has to stand on tiptoes to see above hedges into stubble fields. A timeless air hangs over the narrow street around which Kettlestone clusters, even though there are new houses and plenty of others that have been spruced up.

The church of All Saints lords over a surprisingly cosmopolitan community, possessing an artistic streak that must be the envy of many neighbours, large and small.

This occasion, though, was devoted to home-brewed humour rather than chamber music or watercolours. We crammed into the village hall for a tasty social club menu of sausage and mash, apple pie and old-fashioned spirit.

I had to sing for my supper, but that was no hardship as native and 'blow-in', a jocular description for those working towards a qualification ticket, gossiped, giggled and exchanged good-natured ribbing.

'As in all villages, Kettlestone has its ups and downs, its disagreements and misunderstandings. This sort of event helps unite folk in the best possible way with laughter, nostalgia and wit,' social club chairman Gill Baguley told me.

Well, there were no strangers in that little meeting place, so it's clear a policy of cheerful co-existence is paying off. I'm impressed enough to resist any further temptation to feature Kettlestone on my fantasy list of places ripe for development. Teaset Towers, Crockery Creek, Earl Grey Whistle Test ... leave 'em all on the back boiler and let home-brewed humour work its esteemed wonders.

Signs of home

As the evening sun lit up a patchwork of familiar fields rolling around Red Barn Hill, I knew it would be a happy home-coming.

I pounce on any excuse to nod towards the old family seat at Beeston, despite constant warnings about getting lost in a sea of hemlock, hogweed and a host of halcyon images.

But, as Swaffham woodwork master Harry Carter once told me in a moment of levity, 'to thine own shelf be true'. It was stocked with all the right ingredients on this occasion.

Harry's wisdom and peerless reputation as a carver of local identities in the shape of village signs were easily recalled while we waited for the gathering to grow on the green.

Beeston's new potted history was unveiled by youngsters from the flourishing school just across the road. They told us how the village got its name from a special sort of bent grass, and outlined stories behind features on the sign, from bare-fisted world boxing champion Jem Mace to Liberator planes flown from the nearby base during the last war.

Parish council chairman Brian Potter landed safely with his home-made verses. Vicar Jonathan Boston, happily recovered from serious illness, blessed the sign. We meandered to an impromptu refresh-ments stall outside the village shop. I mardled with relatives and friends, some of them able to match me for distance down yesterday's lokes.

During a little lull, I was convinced I heard Carter's bus approach-ing from Litcham to sweep us all up for a Sunday school outing to Hunstanton or Yarmouth. Reverie was broken by sight of a poster in the shop window advertising a coach trip to Cromer. Good to see the old village going up-market!

Blessed are the sign makers, for they shall light up our parishes. I met the couple who created this new attraction in my old patch. Rodney and Sue Skipper (no relation) also make weather-vanes from their home at Pudding Norton. What points them in this other direction?

Sue has a job in Beeston, and her husband finds time to look after the village war memorial and the green where their latest hand-iwork demands attention. Good to find the Skippers still making a creditable mark!

Just time for a chat and a half at Beeston Ploughshare. No sign of Hugh Grant or the paparazzi, but plenty of intriguing news and views from newcomers and old stagers alike.

The fields around Red Barn Hill slid under night's blanket as I whis-pered farewell. Another successful mid-Norfolk mission to mull over.

'Good job we didn't have to wait for that bus to Cromer...'

◌◌

8 'Foreign' Parts

We have wandered down dusty lanes where haphazard hedges await the reds and rusts of autumn: tiptoed into freshly-harvested fields just to feel and smell the stubble.

Sauntered past snoozing villages, some of them clinging to the coastline for a hint of breeze: celebrated the discovery of a parking space in Southwold, still managing to be polite and well-heeled for all the August invaders.

For the third late summer in a row we have taken up temporary residence in East Suffolk, swapping homes with friends whose rural retreat has long convinced us that life beyond Beccles does have appeal.

Of course, my hard-earned reputation as a tardy traveller has inspired a few more rounds of old favourites like, 'Don't you ever get tired of missionary work?' and 'Not like you to venture abroad!' I remind them that even the twisting road to Uggeshall is paved with good intentions.

Whether these expeditions over the border can release a belated lust for adventure, manifesting itself, perhaps, in a bus trip through darkest Essex, remains to be seen. For the time being I am happy to perambulate gently just a matter of miles from native soil.

The idyllic country base for our family break must betray something of my preoccupation with vast changes on the agricultural scene, particularly at harvest time, since childhood in the middle of Norfolk.

Some may consider it mildly perverse that I should use Suffolk to find echoes of those days before mechanical giants took over to beat and sweep and glean in one mighty roar. A mite ironic, maybe, but certain regrets and thanksgivings know no simple boundaries. I happen to be in Suffolk at the most evocative time of the year for someone raised among shoofs and corn stacks, horses and binders, scores of farming men and family fourses under the hedge.

On the first evening of our holiday, as the sun died gloriously and a little breeze ruffled the taller trees, I stole out alone to laud and lament, to open yesterday's door on today's close-shaved field along the lane.

I chided myself. Sentimental old left-over, chasing imaginary rabbits with a stick! It was nearly dark as I turned away from a canvas Adrian Bell lit so memorably nearly 70 harvests ago:

> *Outside, the moon is up – the harvest moon over harvest fields. It casts a sheen upon the empty stubbles, the bare rounding slopes, so altered from the close-crowed landscape of standing corn. It has glimmering secrets among the trees, and pierces into every entanglement of foliage, and lays faint shadows across the paths.*
> *Each finds a ghost of himself beside him on the ground. An elusive radiance haunts the country; the distances have a sense of shining mist. The men move homeward from the field; the last load creaking up the hill behind them.*

He wrote that as a farmer in Suffolk. I read it again in Suffolk to prove my harvest of memories may not all be tied up with the binder twine of imagination.

Torture on line

A train trip to London could have derailed my ambition to find a natural home on the tolerant wing of the Norfolk branch of Ofsted (Old Fogeys Say Technology Encourages Degeneration).

This was my first capital venture in years, so there were bound to be a few surprises other than failing to take on fresh supplies of coal and water at Stowmarket.

Even so, I was scarcely prepared for the crotchet-crazy crescendo of mobile phones reaching a peak between Colchester and Liverpool Street. With the best will in the world, I could not prevent most callers falling headlong into the first-class posers' compartment.

Inconsequential chunter, from the staggeringly banal 'I'm on the train' and 'Anyone call me?' to what colour a new conservatory planned for the outskirts of Manningtree ought to be, was irritating enough for simple passengers anxious to read or just relax. But the real pain came with a competition to see who could provide the longest and most bizarre variation on the *William Tell* Overture.

Rossini meets Railtrack! Surrealism found a platform on the return leg when seven people dived into and under cases, coats, cartons, cans and newspapers to find out if it was their vital communications tool playing a beckoning tune near Ipswich.

'Hello, what are you lost?' inquired the guard, a regular on the Cromer–Norwich run. Perhaps my bemused look gave him room for concern. It turned out he missed a cultural treat on the final lap of my journey back to the North Norfolk coast.

A devoted young couple boarded at North Walsham. He had a new-fangled portable television set with a very long aerial. She gazed longingly into his eyes as *Top of the Pops* blared out. Yes, I could have moved up or down several places, but I was beyond meaningful protest by this stage.

A fully insulated public transport system may not be possible. Trendybabble with musical overtones must be curbed.

It's good to moan. But who can hear me?

Norfolk links

Looking for Norfolk links is one sure way of keeping the home fires burning when I make the occasional foray into foreign parts.

My visit to the Cotswolds in 1998 yielded a particularly rich harvest concerning parsons, ancient and modern.

Meg, our bustling hostess at Bowden Cottage in the well-groomed Gloucestershire parish of Upton St Leonards, revealed that their vicar had left a year ago 'for a funny-sounding place near the Norfolk coast'.

We ran down the predictable list, headed by Happisburgh, just before our journey ended at Stiffkey. I told her it didn't sound funny at all to me – but that was just familiarity breeding respect. Yes, she had heard all about Harold Davidson, the notorious rector defrocked in the 1930s for displaying a missionary zeal towards fallen women.

'We learned all about him from John before he departed,' said domestic Meg as she presided over the sort to traditional breakfast spread that would have delighted a certain Parson Woodforde.

The Revd John Penny had gone to look after Stiffkey, Cockthorpe, Morston, Langham and Binham. I passed on good wishes from his former parish on my return to Norfolk, and asked for a few instant comparisons.

'The pace of life here is much gentler. Mind you, I was also diocesan press officer during my time at Upton St Leonards, a large village with a busy church, and so had to be ready for all sorts of inquiries.'

My soft probing gave him the chance to preach 'naturalised Norfolk' claims. 'I was previously at All Hallows in Ditchingham, and apart from fairly short spells in Gloucestershire and Yorkshire, I have served in Norfolk since 1979.'

I said we'd talk passports by the end of the century.

The other intriguing connection between the Cotswolds and Norfolk came when my wife picked up a small book in the parish church at Painswick, the town where several of her relatives live.

A Gloucestershire Parson's Wife tells the uplifting story of Agnes Fawcett, who married the local parson, the Revd Charles Neville, in 1814, and did so much to bring hope and order to the neglected hamlet of Sheepscombe, a couple of miles away.

It was a wild and lawless place, the majority of men working at a cloth mill often closed through riotous behaviour fuelled by eight unlicensed ale houses. Mrs Neville inspired new priorities with the building of school, church and parsonage. The Sheepscombe weavers lined up behind the little woman with curly hair gathered under a demure lace cap tied beneath her chin.

It was hardly surprising that her health should fail, and that a move to the bracing Norfolk coast where her husband's family lived was recommended.

Mrs Neville found plenty to do among the Sedgeford poor, organising services in the kitchen of Sedgeford Hall where she and her husband had settled at the invitation of Mr Neville's uncle, who owned it.

In December, 1831, her tenth child was stillborn and Mrs Neville just thirty-six, died a few days later. With the tiny baby in her arms she was buried in the chancel of Sedgeford church.

The Revd Charles Neville succeeded to the family property in Norfolk in 1837. He took the additional name of Rolfe, became vicar as well as squire of Heacham – and died suddenly on Christmas Eve 1852.

Capital chat

Just one small step for Norfolk – but a giant leap for migratory mankind.

A recent train trip to London brought an unexpected chance to reverse that gentrification trend currently lapping around Burnham Market and its well-heeled satellites.

My taxi driver from Liverpool Street to the fleshpots of Camden was a true son of the capital, full of chat, cheek and instant chumminess. I don't think he fully believed me when I claimed I was being head-hunted by a top fashion house keenly interested in the 'buskin look', as well as a string of delicatessens after my secret recipe for marinated coypu. Still, it was a bright morning with an occasional gap in the traffic.

He decided to humour me, extolling the virtues of a provincial life I seemed destined to leave behind. 'Lot of us would like to change places with you, mate.'

I refrained from cheap jibes about a one-sided programme already being in full swing, and inquired where one should contemplate buying a second home in London. 'Keep well away from Islington and Notting Hill. Too fashionable by 'arf. Real locals driven out by rising prices...'

Where on earth have I heard that before? 'You could 'ave a bash at Whitechapel, but I don't suppose it'll be long before they decide Jack the Ripper was just an upwardly mobile geezer who wanted a more respectable neighbourhood.'

Blue plaque material, we agreed, or at least worthy of recognition as a precursor of Home Watch. Then he suggested I might have to settle for a pad outside London altogether. 'That's the way things are going. Just the super-rich left in the middle, and the rest for modest millionaires.' He had a cousin living at Weeting. 'And my muvver-in-law lives near you.' It sounded like a threat. 'Yeh, she says Lincoln is a really nice place. Do you get that way often?'

His patter was better than his geography, but we had discovered an unlikely amount of common ground.

'See you on the Mayfair catwalk!' he cried as I inspected the streets of Camden for traces of gold.

'See you at the next Lincoln broomstick sale!' I retorted, wondering where to go for goat's cheese and spinach flan or something reflecting a Pacific Rim influence.

I ordered a ham roll and a mug of tea instead. Would there be time for a quick visit to Chelsea-Not-On-Sea? No, but I was back on the Norfolk Riviera before 10 o'clock in the evening, musing gently on the way some of the other half live.

Secrets galore

We took the warning as a challenge and, to some degree, a comfort as the Norfolk coastline worked itself up into a late-summer lather.

'It's a genuinely undiscovered area, and they're a bit particular about sharing it with anyone else,' cautioned one guide to Lincolnshire. England's second-largest county, stretching 80 miles from the Humber Bridge in the north to Stamford in the south, was our destination for a family adventure along the bed-and-breakfast trail.

I took a holiday in Sutton Bridge with Uncle Herbert back in the mid-1950s, but I knew little of the land beyond – a matter for some regret as one of Norfolk's nearest neighbours beckoned. Still, many others have ignored what's on their doorsteps.

In a week we could only scratch the top of Lincolnshire's outstandingly fertile soil, sniff the ozone of a coastal belt dominated by gaudy queen Skegness and sample the unexpected variety of the wolds, a continuation of low hills tumbling down from East Yorkshire.

I don't mind steep hills either, so the demanding gradient (with handrail) leading to the oldest and most interesting parts of Lincoln was a trip worth the puffing.

I can't stand heights, so I took a pew and left the wife and lads to climb the tower of St James's at Louth. At 295ft, its spire is the tallest of any parish church in England, while St Botolph's at Boston is the country's fourth-largest parish church and its steeple beats all the rest.

Lonely hamlets under vast skies contrasted uneasily with sudden rashes of development, identical houses crammed on to one small site as if space was at a premium.

A struggle to find overnight accommodation in some parts reinforced the suggestion that Lincolnshire prefers to look after itself rather than woo holidaymakers. For all that, we savoured warm welcomes when we did get fixed up, with farmhouses our favourite ports of call.

A stop at Pigeon Cottage on the outskirts of North Somercotes told us how country life is changing. The proprietor, running adventure holidays for youngsters with his wife as well as a bed-and-breakfast establishment, was up at four in the morning to milk his herd of cows. A dairy farmer forced to diversify to make ends meet.

Lincolnshire tends to revel in comparative obscurity, blessed by good fortune in not being asked to provide the setting for a television series extolling the virtues of a more innocent age.

It is a working county with a few playgrounds by the sea. There is no stereotype image for the marketing boys to exploit, and one suspects any efforts to push the county into fashionable mode would be stoutly resisted.

We liked Lincolnshire enough to want to go back for a longer look. Perhaps that cussed streak lends extra appeal.

Dialect hero

This postcard from Dorset comes trimmed with most of the traditional ingredients ... sun-dappled hills, chocolate-box villages, dramatic stretches of coastline, Tolpuddle Martyrs and Thomas Hardy's cottage. Even so, our family journey along the bed-and-breakfast trail was dominated by a search for one of my heroes, William Barnes, the Dorset dialect poet.

While he is not entirely a prophet without honour in his own county, and one of the very few dialect writers to make a national mark, Barnes yet awaits the full flowering of acknowledgement.

His statue stands in the centre of Dorchester, next door to the impressive county museum of which he was a founding father.

There is a William Barnes Society and one of his best poems, 'Linden Lea', was set to music by Ralph Vaughan Williams at the beginning of the twentieth century.

The self-taught parson poet earned his place among the towering figures of Victorian literature. Tennyson, Hardy and Gerard Manley Hopkins looked upon him as an equal. Indeed, Hardy called Barnes 'a lyric writer of a high order of genius'.

His glossary of the Dorset dialect, first compiled in 1844, underlined how the speech he had heard in the Blackmore Vale of his youth was disappearing in the face of urbanisation and standardisation. He went to great lengths to set down a faithful record of what it had once been.

Like John Clare before him, Barnes proved there could be a market for good rustic verse, and you didn't have to be soaked in Dorset ways to understand it. A commendable plus, still attracting new admirers.

For all these achievements and plaudits, a highly ambivalent attitude revealed on his death in 1886 lingers to this day. I found few in his home town of Sturminster Newton ready to offer 'favourite son' status, while gentle probing around Dorset betrayed an alarming level of ignorance about him and his work.

A small attendance at his funeral was soon outweighed by the formation of a memorial committee, moved to serious action by the Bishop of Salisbury after a poor start. Over 90 dignitaries then clamoured to be appointed. Dorchester's first statue went up.

Edwardian surgeon Sir Frederick Treves summed up 'this tardy act of grace' when he recalled 'the folk of Dorchester ignored him while he lived and only honoured him when he had passed beyond the sound of their applause'.

Perhaps many found his passion for dialect, springing from a humble background, more a matter for patronising nods rather than wholehearted approbation.

Perhaps the bicentenary of his birth in 2001 will be marked by a new wave of appreciation, culminating in the formation of a long overdue Dorset Dialect Society.

William Barnes is too important to be locked away in one county. But it is up to Dorset to make much more of his talents to help inspire a national crusade in the name of our beleaguered dialects.

Book paradise

Our recent family safari, centred on the Cotswolds and Wye Valley, must dispel once and for all this ridiculous notion that I am reluctant to leave Norfolk's homely bosom.

I lasted a whole week away without begging to be brought back, comforted to some extent by discovering how most other places have to endure too much traffic and noise, silly property prices, mobile-phone mania and occasional shop assistants who cannot talk or add up.

By the time we reached the Welsh Borders, all hills and sheep, twisty lanes and lovely views, my withdrawal symptoms had surrendered completely to old-fashioned excitement.

Hay-on-Wye, paradise for bookworms, spoke volumes to me under sultry skies of tourism and good taste being compatible. Sadly, I drew a blank in the search for East Anglian writers like James Blyth, Mary Mann and Harold Freeman.

Nor were there any flickers of recognition or offers to go looking for them when I mentioned their names in about 20 shops. They put me down as a Norfolk nomad with eccentric tastes.

The other major disappointment of our tour concerned the treasures of Hereford Cathedral. I have written to the Dean to underline feelings shared by several other visitors on the day.

We took to heart an immediate invitation to consider a £2 donation from each of our family group of four towards the upkeep of this glorious building. We patronised the gift shop and café, and the lads treated themselves to a trip up the tower.

We wanted to round it all off with a close up of the Mappa Mundi and Chained Library, two of our most important historical treasures now exhibited together at the west end of the cathedral.

We balked at an admission price of £10 for a family ticket, the cheapest option on offer.

A sting too far in this pay-as-you-go tale. We refused to fork out the best part of £20 just to look around Lincoln Cathedral a couple of years back. Frankly, I think this whole grasping business is getting out of hand.

Entrance to all places of worship should be free. Viewing of items like a spectacular medieval map of the world ought to be actively encouraged, especially among the young, not subjected to prohibitive price fixing.

Left to their own instincts, I'm sure the majority of cathedral visitors would be 'generous to a vault'.

What they object to at present is having collection boxes rattled constantly under their noses.

Now for a few holiday plus points, apart from the weather which held firm until the last leg of our journey home between Wisbech and Cromer. The A47 did a fair impression of a river in full flow.

I warmed to Coventry Cathedral, modern and uplifting, for giving me the rare chance to employ those two adjectives together.

Kenilworth Castle, that glorious ruin of Elizabethan England, sent out fascinating reminders of Robert Dudley, poor Amy Robsart and far-reaching Norfolk connections.

Ross-on-Wye welcomed 'home' my wife to St Mary's parish church where her parents were married and she and her brother were christened.

A super-charged collie dog called Red and a droll Australian entomologist called Mark kept the boys entertained at our idyllic farmhouse bed-and-breakfast stop near Hay-on-Wye.

Another rural retreat was to be found at Barford, near Warwick, with the Joseph Arch pub standing out in his home village. A pioneer of the farm workers' union movement, along with our own George Edwards, Joseph later became MP for North West Norfolk.

Swarming with visitors, Stratford-on-Avon inspired puckish lines like 'Where there's a Will, there's a crowd', 'A Bard in the hand is worth two in the rush' and 'Thank God we don't go this barmy over Nelson!'

The Dean replies:

The Dean of Hereford Cathedral has responded swiftly to my complaints after a family visit to this splendid building.

As stated, we accepted the suggestion to make a donation of £2 apiece on arrival. We patronised the gift shop and café. The boys paid themselves for a trip up the tower.

I wrote to the dean explaining that we felt £10 too much to see the other treasures, underlining deep disappointment at this 'sting too far', a feeling evidently shared by a stream of other disgruntled visitors who refused to pay an extra £4 a head to see the treasures.

The Very Revd Michael Travinor says he does understand how a family day out can prove very expensive.

'It may well be that we can find some way of explaining likely costs of the whole visit before people enter the cathedral.

'I should mention, however, that at Hereford we have two major attractions on the same site, an ancient cathedral with high costs of upkeep and the famous Mappa Mundi, with its own costs for upkeep and conservation. Somehow we need to enable people to give realistically to both if they wish to visit both,' said the Dean. He agrees with me that admission to all places of worship should be free. 'This is the case at Hereford, and we feel able only to suggest a possible level of donation. This is in no way to be seen as an admission charge.'

Point taken – but the 'invitation' on entry is in fairly bold letters, certainly big enough to follow reluctant contributors all the way round! As for my suggestion that the bulk of cathedral visitors would be as generous as possible if left to their own instincts, the Dean provides a telling riposte:

'When I was at Ely Cathedral, and we left the donations entirely to people's discretion, the average giving was 12p per person. I rather think if we gave no guidance at Hereford we would get rather the same result.'

I am surprised at such a meagre figure, but that does not alter the general tone of my criticism. The Dean of Hereford has promised to explore more fully the issue of how his cathedral communicates costs and needs to visitors. A tacit acceptance perhaps, that a major public relations exercise is needed.

∽

9 Deeper Musings

An old man of the Norfolk soil set me guessing back in the 1950s when he basked in 'mellowsun days.'

It took a while to work out what he meant. I thought at first he was talking about 'medicine' or 'Nelson' as he rolled out words and phrases in broad dialect tones.

Then it dawned on me. He peered skywards, shielded his eyes as if in salute to an all-conquering power and undid another button on his waistcoat.

He was paying tribute to a glorious spell of weather after the corn harvest. I shouldn't have been surprised at such lyrical language. He and several contemporaries echoed Shakespeare when hailing the sun as 'bright Phoebus in his strength'.

That old man's wonderful feel for words returned to keep me company on blackberry-picking expeditions in a warm glow surrounding the end of September and the start of October.

'Mellowsun days' sums up perfectly a gentle tour of North Norfolk lanes in search of bounty for jams, pies and crumbles … as well as to find renewed faith in our beleaguered countryside.

My wife and lads call these hedgerow raids my 'annual fix', hinting at a tender but obvious obsession with the past. I admit to hearing the squeals and feeling the scratches of boyhood as I strain to reach the plumpest clusters still hanging defiantly out of reach.

There are plenty of Norfolk yesterdays to fill a basket along a quiet byway where traffic is rare and a pheasant's chortle takes top billing for sound effects. Stubble glints, dragonflies dart and giant cobwebs tickle your face and hands as you enter the larder.

Yes, there is unfading romance attached to this pastoral scene, notwithstanding an undoubted crisis in farming, a crisis which ought to prompt The Great Countryside Mooch after The Great Countryside March.

While urban dwellers stand accused of simply failing to understand country life – they think it's all rosy-cheeked rustics spreading thick fresh butter over crusty loaves while Rover rounds up the cows – it's worth asking an awkward question or two nearer home.

How many people attending harvest festivals in Norfolk have set a foot inside a harvest field this year? How many residents from any four Norfolk villages picked at random would be able to chat easily about agricultural topics with a local farmer?

Let's be honest. Not all barriers are built in Whitehall and Westminster. We create several of our own in what is still a predominantly agricultural county.

A small beginning, perhaps, but thousands might benefit from a few quiet minutes beside a hedge dripping with autumn ripeness: out of the car, down a lane to remember the difference between hips and haws and to see how one harvest hands over to another.

'Mellowsun days' will be gone too soon.

Arcadian longings

When I was a lad, and much closer to the Norfolk soil than I am now, it was easy to be in awe of farmers.

They owned all that land and property. They provided work for many people in the locality, numbers rising dramatically for the sugar beet and corn harvests.

Yes, there was a whiff of feudalism lingering over our rural scene, especially where families lived in tied cottages which went with the jobs. Wages were poor alongside those on offer in town and city.

But farmers who treated their acres and workers with genuine respect brought a sense of security to a pastoral picture destined to change beyond recall within a couple of decades.

It may be too simple to cite mechanisation and the Common Agricultural Policy as main reasons for the revolution, but we know button-pushing and form-filling now take precedence over muck-spreading and crop-tilling.

Farmers are on the march to draw attention to an industry struggling to keep its head above the headlands. Leaving aside any details of what happened when angry employees tried that one themselves in the name of family survival, most notably in the 1920s, I admit my awe has turned to sympathy.

Falling farm incomes must affect the rural economy as a whole. Only one brick in the wall, I know, but a continuing decline in fortunes will encourage the surrender of many more precious green acres for house-building. There are plenty of developers rubbing their hands in anticipation.

Diversification of recent years, golf courses, farm shops and holiday cottages leading the way, told us the old order had gone. But that did not prepare us for the possibility of a countryside without a soul at the end of the twentieth century.

At the heart of this dilemma are farmers, many of them ploughing an old family furrow, who know it is only a matter of time before they have to leave the land.

To whom? More executive dwellers who want to play pretend gentry? Fresh hordes of trippers seeking respite from the rigours and stresses of urban life? Grasping builders backed by a government who denounced a frightening development tide when they were in opposition and alarmed by the let-rip policies of the likes of Nicholas Ridley?

Whatever we think of the present generation of 'custodians of the countryside', I fear the next will be mighty short on compassion, commitment and conservation. Agri-business and concrete mixers have no truck with such niceties.

For all the deep-rooted problems, and threats of more to come, Arcadian longings will continue to add peculiar pressures of their own. A rural fantasy, fed by Whitehall mandarins and Westminster politicians confronted with unreasonable demands for new homes in the country, simply remains too useful to put to flight.

Making a fetish out of the rural and the rustic whets appetites and sells houses. Fewer experienced and successful farmers to counter such arrant nonsense leaves another gate open to the voracious field-eaters.

The heritage bug

I have been dubious about selling our heritage on the burgeoning holiday market ever since a visit to Camelot Country in 1984.

King Arthur and his legends of many locations had given rise to a massive tourist campaign, not least around Tintagel in Cornwall with its castle ruins and echoes of paradise lost.

Rip-off merchants were busy merging old and new. Merlin's Disco was just the place for exercise after a good blow-out at the Holy Grill. Lancelot's Laundrette, Galahad's Gifts, Excalibur Excursions and Guinevere's Takeaway … the golden goose honked at every turn.

A local writer told me, 'We see nothing now but the commercial exploitation of these myths. It is the achievement of the twentieth century to turn a poem into a bazaar.'

He expressed sincere hopes that places like Norfolk, with a growing holiday trade, would take careful note of the Arthurian circus and so avoid such blatant excesses.

I suggested Mawther of the Pit could never match for poetry the Lady of the Lake, and returned home chastened to keep a beady eye on fluctuating shares in Black Shuck Enterprises.

Frankly, Norfolk and the majority of visitors it attracts do not appear to have been bitten too badly by the heritage bug. Selling our souls for a mass of pottery is not commonplace.

But a word of warning must be in order after revelations that the county's favourite son is to be marketed and packaged in the guise of a teddy bear.

Admiral Lord Nelson, most brilliant and most honoured naval leader Britain has known, is to be prepared for the task of providing 'a more welcoming image of Norfolk in that he will identify the cuddly, hospitable side that is underneath the Norfolk mentality'.

Oh, that has to be the side Lady Hamilton came to know and love once he had loosened up with a swig of Burnham grog and a few earthy Norfolk yarns picked up from press-gang concerts on the *Victory.*

Our caution is often mistaken for coldness, our independence confused with indifference. If Nelson Teddy can blow those out of the crow's nest of stereotypes, his dressing-up will not have been in vain.

Trouble is, unscrupulous folk will take liberties – like a Norfolk free marketeer, who deliberately thought the cuddly creation was to be christened Nelson Eddy… 'Great! Now we need a Lady Hamilton doll able to sing like Jeanette McDonald. They could team up and do for Trafalgar what Abba did for Waterloo. Get me their agents on the hornblower!'

You can guess at some other delights in store … Boadicea wheelie bins (without the knives), Parson Woodforde diet sheets, George Edwards crow-scarers, Humphrey Repton garden makeovers, Henry Blogg wave machines, Robert Kett pet enclosures, Thomas Paine time-shares, Black Shuck burglar alarms…

Norfolk expects every man to pursue his booty. But not at the risk of pricing everything and valuing nothing.

Guests from history

With wind and sleet railing against window and calendar, I have every excuse to draw the curtains and prepare for one of my occasional candlelit suppers.

'Oh, to be in Norfolk now that April's here...' was the general theme for discussion among a small but select group of guests culled from history's pages.

They were invited not only in the name of excellent company and conversation but also in fond belief they could make some sense of being placed in a completely different era. They did not disappoint.

Clement Scott was amused at the thought of discovering daffodil-land over a century of seasons after first falling under the spell of crumbling cliffs and fields dotted with poppies.

As in August, 1883, he arrived in Cromer by train, but this time chose not to pack sandwiches and go rambling towards Sidestrand and the Garden of Sleep.

'Those lazy old winds go straight through one!' he chortled as we chatted about everything from dressed crabs to stressed motorists, chilly economic draughts to global warming. He seemed to accept that bathing machines had gone for good.

Scott saw Poppyland turn into Bungalowland. Now he is tempted to call it Caravanland, but retains deep affection for an area he made fashionable among London's literary and artistic set. 'It can still inspire verses as well as holiday brochures,' he mused ... with just a hint of guilt.

Robert Kett was intrigued to hear tanners had gone out of circulation as a result of decimalisation, but he was sure his home town of Wymondham could still 'jangle the coinage of rebellion when needed'.

He, too, travelled to Cromer by rail from Norwich, and was dumb-founded to see what had happened to the site of his last stand against the Earl of Warwick's superior forces in a low valley just north of the city.

'Forsooth, Dussindale is on the march to Rackheath!' he announced with mock solemnity before asking how many tanners it would take to pay for an executive dwelling not far from his beloved Mousehold Heath.

Kett was pleased to learn how, four-and-a-half centuries after being hanged for treason, he was regarded as a noble and courageous leader in the struggle of the common people to escape from a servile life.

'Time mellows reputations. Let us hope it does the same for extensive brickwork,' he mused.

Mary Mann was surprised to discover some problems highlighted in her books at the turn of the twentieth century were still rising above Norfolk's fertile headlands.

Rural plight rather than rustic charm ... an essential thread running through harrowing stories, including *The Fields of Dulditch*, her most celebrated, first published in 1902 and based on her experiences as a squire's wife in the isolated village of Shropham.

Brutality and poverty dominated labourers' lives, but she did not ignore serious troubles confronting landowners. For example, her novel *Moonlight* opened with the suicide of a bankrupt farmer.

She said her journey to our coastal gathering had suggested 'prosperous lives in an attractive and well-managed countryside'. Calendar pictures surrendered to grim facts about crisis after crisis cropping up to belie pastoral calm.

Shrinking incomes, dwindling facilities and distant indifference are none too obvious to a passing glance.

Our candlelit supper continued long into the Norfolk night. Still, tourism, development and agriculture make up the sort of menu it is impossible to make light of in any age.

Traffic and yobs

Norfolk towns are awash with the revival spirit. Sadly, my brothers and sisters, the hallelujahs could be hollow.

Hardly a day passes without another scheme being launched on the back of ready cash designed to regenerate our larger communities.

All are well-intentioned. Some are highly ambitious. A few are already testing that old local reputation for dogged resistance to radical change, like a pavement-widening programme in the middle of Cromer's narrow thoroughfare. All are likely to founder unless long-term solutions can be applied to the twin terrors striking at the very fabric of these places – infestations of traffic by day and yobs at night.

This is not scaremongering or cocking a snook at hardy souls bidding to better the quality of life around us. It is simple acceptance of irrefutable evidence on both counts after decades of walking the streets in my home county.

As a non-driver, I may be biased against cars, especially in residential and built-up areas, but I have witnessed at close range the sort of degeneration in mood and movement that defies denial.

Our town centres have become dangerous and dirty, noisy and congested, and no infusion of money can spell improvement unless it is matched by genuine moves to cut down traffic.

Then, brighter shops and relaxed shoppers will bring real revival, and so stifle calls for more edge-of-town developments cynically proposed to take advantage of chaos in the middle.

Anti-social behaviour in our town centres after dark, often fuelled by drink and drugs, has reduced many residents to part-time roles. They draw the curtains and call it a day around 5pm.

I was in Sheringham for a Friday evening function a few weeks ago, guest of one of the town's favourite sons, renowned for his humour, tolerance and charitable attitude towards folk of all kinds and all ages.

We ran the gauntlet of about a dozen youngsters brandishing cans and bottles of booze, as if in some archaic rite to announce their acceptance into a specific warring tribe. It was just after 10 o'clock. My friend suggested this was a gentle rehearsal for regular late-night disturbances he could see and hear from his home.

'There's little the police can do. The parents clearly don't care. My wife and I don't come out after dark very often because we feel threatened, and that's a dreadful thing to admit in a small town where we've lived all our lives.'

There's no consolation to be gleaned from predictable claims that choking traffic and intimidating behaviour are even worse in other places. It's Norfolk hearts they're breaking round here.

Regeneration must address truly difficult issues if it wants to be taken seriously. Pots of money and pots of paint may help. But it will take much more to redeem the souls of Norfolk towns.

Speaking volumes

While I could be talked into accepting that some people really do benefit from owning mobile phones, I refuse point-blank to regard recent sights and sounds in Cromer as anything but ridiculous posturing.

Sadly, the folk involved appeared inordinately pleased with their very public performances.

None could be described as young and trendy, tailor-made for the latest fashion accessories. All were holidaymakers, as I could tell by their voices, casual clothing, subject matter and mannerisms.

Before I am accused of being a voyeur with tourist-bashing and machine-smashing tendencies, let me emphasise these incidents came to me during normal rounds of mixing business with pleasure. I did not go looking or listening for them.

A middle-aged man in floral shirt and baggy shorts used his trusty mobile phone to boom out an order to one of Cromer's splendid fish and chip shops. He was less than 50 yards from the establishment – and probably called the North Sea a couple of minutes later to ask if the cod were fresh.

I made my regular trek to the end of Cromer Pier, one of Norfolk's top refuges for those who put bracing air and taking it slowly high on a list of priorities.

There stood a man at the entrance to the lifeboat shed, putting his wife in the picture. She was in Doncaster.

I gathered as much when he asked about the weather back home. He had the cheek to suggest it was very quiet on the North Norfolk coast. I wanted to tell him it was usually much quieter, but his high-decibel antics continued as I headed back down the pier.

My third instalment of mobile phone philistinism occurred in the doorway of Cromer parish church. A couple took turns to tell some bright culinary spark at the other end what ingredients were needed for a sponge cake.

Such a surrealistic episode raised fears of another call regarding oven temperature and baking time as they mooched among the pews. Happily, the call never came. Perhaps there was divine interference on the line.

No, I am not a Luddite with attitude. But many more loud exhibitions from people who have forgotten what it is like to feel embarrassed could send me into serious training.

End of another season

Seagulls squeal and wheel in disappointment over a sudden slump in the titbits takeaway service.

A fitful sun scribbles plaintive shadows on shifting blue-grey waters while a dog sniffs lazily round a plastic bottle on the promenade.

There are more tractors than trippers on the beach, more boats than bathers, more crumpled cartons than freshly created castles.

A melancholy air flaps at a poster advertising the last Sunday concert at the end of the pier. End of season. Start of long lull before crowds return.

'Nice to have the place back to ourselves,' declares the fifth familiar figure you recognise in as many minutes. No discernible guilt in the voice despite the proximity of lingering visitors well armed with headscarves, rain hats, wind-cheaters and defiant chins.

Sea-front shops muster a final wink at potential customers before boards go up. Café waitresses squeeze another smile out of the teapot as they sweeten farewells with a hopeful 'See you next year.'

Everywhere smells a little of decay, sadness, chilliness and goodbye. Everyone walks and talks at a more measured pace. Everything seems to be tied up in crispness at either end of shortening days.

There is no bold line between summer calendar and autumn almanac, just a gradual turn of colour and mood. Indeed, on a bright, mild October morning, our seaside can be far more exciting than at season's congested peak.

Now, all these mellow reflections as the year grows old could be at variance with prolonged talk of coastal regeneration. For some, cosy musings on the virtues of Cromer's reputation as an enduring beacon of consistency in a boiling sea of change are both misplaced and outdated.

While I line up regularly with traditionalists urging extreme caution in embracing 'progress' for its own sake, usually coated in sugary words about 'economic benefits', I am prepared to make a few concessions.

As a microcosm of Norfolk, fighting valiantly to marry old and new in a tasteful and temperate way, Cromer has to stop feeling guilty about accepting spruce-up money from outside. After all, there's no apparent conscience at relieving visitors of their loot during the summer months.

This must be the way ahead for small resorts to keep them afloat all year round. And here's an even better idea to simplify and perhaps settle that long-running argument over edge-of-town development.

Any business aiming for fringe benefits should be actively encouraged … as long as it agrees to set up a 'twin' branch in the town centre. An obvious boost for Cromer's ailing heart and a perfect guide to any impact extra outlets on the outskirts may have on the traditional trading area.

See, I do think seriously about these mattes while taking the autumn air along Cromer Pier. At least there's no need to waste money or time on alterations to this priceless asset.

10 Lighter Moments

Hi. Join me on the mean streets of Cromer as a burst of November sun apologises for poking its nose into another season's business.

Trippers gone, but traffic growls on. Pigeons fill the skies, and decorate the pavements. 'Coo dirtat' mutters the town linguist without waiting for applause. He knows the shortcomings of a throwaway society.

The day starts well. I clear the office window on the inside with at tissue left limp by a nautical client's salty tears, and ask myself if Norfolk spiders ought to have their own website. A positive response proves the art of condensation is not dead.

'Down-at-heel gumshoe solves international mystery' is just one of the headlines missing as I flick through my newspaper and wait for the phone to burble. My old friend Inspector Migraine at Interpal is due to call from his plush new garret on the Rue d'Awakening.

I promise myself not to mention beef casseroles, apple dumplings, lamb stew or a recent dream about General de Gaulle looking like a llama surprised in its bath. Easy to keep promises when the phone never rings.

I leave Poppyland Investigations to its fourth-floor reverie and head for the patch where human foibles, failings and frustrations fall over each other to be noticed. A walk back from Sheringham is uplifting.

My contact on the pier has no news of the Matlaske Falcon. But he may have a fresh lead on the Hound of the Basketmeals. 'Shucks!' I cry excitedly. He turns white and turns away, making light of the upward trek into town.

I spot him later in a speakeasy masquerading as a luncheon club for the over-eighties. 'If you don't leave, I'll get someone who will,' he whispers. I get outside just in time to see a purple evening ready to pick a fight with itself over West Runton.

Cynics will say another day wasted, another bit of grit in a rheumy private eye, another hole in the sole of a scruffy gumshoe. But I know the value of keeping all boulevards open.

These are my streets, my people. We may be short of a few mansions with wedding-cake decorations and double dormer windows and a Rolls-Royce Silver Wraith or Chrysler Sedan living outside. We do have each other as the ozone slayer gathers spite and screams abuse at all pigeons who have aspirations to be second homers.

I'll be on the case, the biggest challenge of an exacting coastal career, watching and waiting for vital clues when bitter winds roar in from the old German Ocean.

Just how will mobile phone posers cope with all those critical calls on the hoof after earmuffs, balaclavas, flying helmets, fur caps, sou'westers and Nora Batty headscarves have taken over as real fashion accessories?

'Pidgin power' mutters the town linguist without daring to wait for applause. He knows I can apply the coo de grass whenever the entente cordiale runs out.

Cultural treat

Norfolk culture has been subjected to countless influences in recent times, not least by the number of lucky people moving in to live among us and the Mummerzet brigade making a mockery of the accent in drama productions on television and radio.

So, to help reinforce the county's firm commitment to dew diffrunt despite all pressures towards dull uniformity, I have prepared a Norfolk Culture Lovers' ABC. It should prove invaluable at crucial times in upper circles, especially on visits to the theatre when it is de rigeur to stand out from the crowd:

A is for Aylsham Treat – that's treating yourself. Saves a lot of arguments over which opera to attend.

B is for Buskins – shiny leather gaiters ideal for protection against enthusiastic newcomers to line dancing.

C is for Chummy – a soft felt hat with narrow brim to wear with pride on opening nights.

D is for Dodman – friendly snail ready to overtake the Norfolk theatre-goer on his way to buy a round at the bar.

E is for Ewe – past tense of 'owe' to prove all debts have been settled before an expensive evening out.

F is for Furriner – probably the person sitting next to you in the increasingly cosmopolitan world of entertainment.

G is for Garp – a long stare from that person next to you as you glory in the Norfolk vernacular. Just smile back.

H is for Horkey – social gathering to celebrate the end of harvest. Vicars often attend for the free beer.

I is for Iceni – they set a useful example when it came to sorting out furriners (q.v.). Boadicea patented the wheelie-bin with knives.

J is for Jam – to walk heavily or stamp on. Just mind that furriner's toes when you go for an ice cream.

K is for Knockin' an' toppin' – main topic for discussion among farm workers during the interval.

L is for Larn – eternal search for enlightenment, on and off stage. If you make your first visit to the theatre, that'll larn yer!

M is for Mardle – a leisurely chat best saved for half-time, although it can come in useful if the performance is lacklustre.

N is for Noffin' – what most mardles (q.v.) amount to when you are just being polite and waiting for the resumption.

O is for On the sosh – one of Norfolk's colourful descriptions for something on the slant. Can apply to scenery after a rousing dance or clumsy entrance.

P is for Plawks – the hand you put together in appreciation of the best show you've seen in years. Especially if you got in for nothing.

Q is for Quackle – to choke or half-strangle. Perhaps you are not used to dressing up and wearing a tight collar, but familiarity will come.

R is for Rum ole dew – a perfect description for any show celebrating the best of Norfolk culture.

S is for Squit – our most precious commodity in a world that wants to take itself much too seriously. Shorthand for Norfolk culture.

T is for Tizzick – a troublesome cough three rows back that could well lead to suffin' goin' about, Norfolk's most common ailment.

U is for Useter – as in 'I uster go ter the pub every night, but now I hev Friday's orf ter trosh down the theatre.'

V is for Ventriloquist – a deliberate omission from any theatrical line-up as Norfolk purists refuse to put words into other people's mouths.

W is for Weskit – a garment worn to the theatre in honour of the great playwright who put Norfolk on the map with *Roots*.

X is for Xenophobia – a word no Norfolk culture lover can pronounce or understand. Leave smart explanations to the furriners.

Y is for Yisty – the day you'll be telling them about tomorrow as you reflect on an unforgettable theatrical experience.

Z is for Zackly – Exactly! And thass zackly right we should salute Norfolk's desire to always dew diffrunt.

Horkey spread

There was more shadow than sunlight on the wheat as it rustled and swayed in tune with a lively breeze. My bike groaned up the hill.
I arrived safely at the Gathered Inn for a meeting to discuss the horkey, our annual social gathering and feast to celebrate end of harvest.

First item on the agenda, inevitably, was to call on retired farm worker Josiah Tizzick for a brief outline of traditions behind the event. He was on his sturdy Norfolk feet for just over two hours.

We guessed he might be reaching the end of his rustic sermon when he took a long pull from his tankard, sleeve-wiped froth from his beard and burst into the third verse of 'To Be A Farmer's Boy', a subtle hint he would like to be included on the entertainment menu for the seventy-eighth successive year.

Committee chairman Arthur Buskin said it was now imperative to scythe through other items in time to get instructions to Rosy Biffin and her team of willing workers for the famous horkey spread.

It was agreed to ask for the same again, although Ernie Highlow said he didn't want little lumps of hard bread floating on top of his coypu soup, and Eric Morfrey wondered if a selection of local cheeses could include Wendlingdale and Cheddargrave.

Landlord 'Rum'un' Rimer offered to look after the bar as the function was being held in the upstairs room of the Gathered Inn for the seventy-eighth successive year. He noted requests for two firkins of Castle Riesling for the main toast.

'Dunt want no bloomin speechifyin!' barked Josiah Tizzick, threatening to break into the fourth verse of a well-known rural anthem. He won support from Lady Amelia Coombe-Yellums, anxious to be invited to read her favourite Boy John letter to the assembled company and to tell the one earthy joke in her repertoire, about the parrot and the parson.

The Revd 'Happy' Hutkin agreed to say grace and also provide a benediction for anyone still capable of listening at the end. He said Mrs Hutkin would be pleased to bake the harvest sheaf if someone would be good enough to tell her what one looked like. 'We call it a shoof!' exclaimed Josiah Tizzick.

That just left the VIP guest list and seating arrangements, with no need to remind organisers that the Highlows and the Morfreys have not spoken since the wet harvest of 1927. Trouble flared over who sat on which sacks in the barn to eat their potted meat sandwiches.

'Do we need a famous personality?' inquired Arthur Buskin. 'Blarst, cors we dunt!' muttered Josiah Tizzick. Even so, the chairman called for suggestions from the floor. The woman from Hairpin Cottage wondered if that nice Jeremy Clarkson was free on that date and fancied a trip to Norfolk.

No one else had heard of him. In any event, said Lady Amelia, there would be no room for additional parking outside the pub after all the tractors had come in from the farms and the fields.

So, our harvest horkey will rely, as usual, on home-made entertainment with a Farmer's Boy, the Boy John and a well-loved story featuring the parrot and the parson topping the bill.

My bike wheezed down the hill. There was more shadow than moonlight on the wheat as it rustled. I swayed in time with a lively breeze.

Songs of praise

These are changing times for the small but fervent congregation at St Mawkin's-on-the-Sosh.

'Better happy-clappy than grumpy-thumpy!' is the inspirational text pinned to the oak door of this ivy-clad fourteenth-century church set in open fields on the outskirts of the scattered parish of Blackstalk Parva.

The Revd Garfield 'Otis' Reading, in charge of this and eight other rural gems, took over a year ago after starting his career in Sheffield and making an impact with his 'Stir it with the curate' mid-week services.

These were notable for their informality, pots of tea being shared during his sermons and washing-up duties carried out in the font before the final hymn. 'I wanted people to feel at home, to forget they were in a draughty old building, but to relax and unwind.'

He admitted to being surprised when so many parishioners brought sleeping bags, ghetto-blasters, cocktail cabinets, mobile phones, frozen meals and laptop computers to church, but said they had to keep up with trends in city, town and country.

'Our Lord would have used the Internet to spread the message, and the streets of Nazareth must surely have been dug for cables.'

What about St Mawkin's-on-the-Sosh? "The people are setting the agenda, and I have been truly uplifted by their capacity to embrace change as well as each other. We have only one Sunday service a month, so it is imperative to make it memorable."

What about that traditional Norfolk reserve? 'Out of sight! My three regulars at Blackstalk Parva voted immediately to get rid of the Victorian harmonium and the strait-jacket of rigid propriety that has bedevilled country worship for centuries. Now there are rumours of Major and Mrs Stannickle-Hulver returning to the fold. Hallelujah!'

What about multitudes lining up against 'rave in the nave' antics? 'We must pray for them, convert them and remind them that Norfolk has led the path to glory before.' He noted my mystified look.

'A century ago you may recall how Jeremiah Colman launched the Carrowsmatic Movement for his mustard factory workers. Did not this most benevolent of employers, a real father of his people, set new standards?

'Then came the Company of Shakers to put new life into our rural churches during the 1920s. They were a Norfolk offshoot of the Quivering Brethren based in Sussex...'

It all came back to me. 'Come, my son, and join us this Sunday at St Mawkin's-on-the-Sosh. Judge for yourself. Find balm in a psalm!'

I'm off across the fields to see and hear the new evangelical zeal in action.

Swinging flock

At the behest of the parson, the Revd Garfield 'Otis' Reading, I duly attended Sunday morning worship at St Mawkin's-on-the-Sosh.

I could hear banging, thumping and stamping as I crossed the wide and lonely field to this small fourteenth-century church on the outskirts of the scattered parish of Blackstalk Parva.

The regular congregation were taking off muddy boots and trying to keep warm in the porch. All three shuddered as they embraced me. I walked past the font full of live bait and sat beneath a loudspeaker installed just above a damp patch bearing a close resemblance to a map of Borneo.

The trio skipped to their instruments. A short, portly woman fondled her sackbut. A tall, thin man organised his serpent. An elderly lady I recognised as Esme Porter, harmonium player and chief flower arranger at the church since 1929, hugged her lyre.

We sang an upbeat version of 'Wake, O Wake, For Night is Flying', although I made little musical headway with a tambourine thrust into my hands.

The door creaked open and Major and Mrs Stannickle-Hulver strode purposefully to the family pew as our chorus ended. They had returned to the fold. The Major carried a large torch borrowed from his gamekeeper, and his wife clutched a big rattle more at home on a football terrace.

They remained standing as a fanfare blared from the loudspeaker above the contour of Borneo. The Revd Garfield 'Otis' Reading emerged from the vestry. He punched the air, smiled broadly and waved to the couple who have come home.

'Put a strobe on the robe!' exclaimed the Major, letting his light so shine to dazzling effect.

'Try a reacher for the preacher!' enthused his wife as she extended her arms, creased her two-piece and twirled her rattle.

'Come alive with a tithe!' called the tall, thin man, pushing his serpent aside and picking up the collection plate.

We sang one verse of 'Mark, A Hundred Notes are Swelling', and Esme Porter played a few on her lyre as it was her week for a solo spot.

The Revd Garfield 'Otis' Reading said he did not preach sermons but simply 'cosied up' to his friends and equals.

He scoffed at 'Corn-again Christians' who attend church only at harvest festival time, warned us to beware all politicians' blandishments in the next few weeks and promised to respect all those with more traditional tastes at St Mawkin's-on-the-Sosh.

'Bless thee, old partner! See you at the harvest festival!' he smiled as I left.

The rest of his flock were singing and swaying beneath the map of Borneo.

Potty plunge

In the good old days, when we had proper winters, I suffered from chilblains. Too much toe-toasting in front of a coal fire, followed by bedtime bliss with a hot-water bottle, aggravated the ailment.

One of our neighbours, far more concerned about the health of his vegetable plot than my suffering feet, betrayed his sense of priorities when he exclaimed: 'Cor, blarst me, if I hed radishes like that, I'd take first prize at the local show!'

Various ointments were tried, but the majority of more sympathetic friends and relations assured me the only real solution hid under my bed. Dipping chilblains in a chamber-pot of fresh urine became a regular means of easing the pain.

I don't know if taking pot luck brought genuine curing qualities to the surface, but earnest advice came from too many quarters to dismiss it as a load of old squit. And my toes did seem to be soothed by this bedroom exercise.

Memories have been stirred by a fascinating miscellany put together by members and volunteers at the Wayland Hall Care Centre in Watton.

A section on old-fashioned remedies includes the chamber-pot treatment for chilblains, as tried and tested by Gail Adcock, hostess at the centre and main force behind the booklet.

Florence Nurse recalls rubbing onion juice on chilblains, a remedy echoed in *Full Circle*, Dick Joice's memoirs published in 1991. The popular Anglia TV presenter included several items from *Grandma's Commonplace Book*, a cure for chilblains reading: 'Cut top off onion, dip into salt and rub well into affected parts. Paraffin or turpentine could be similarly used.'

Gabrielle Hatfield's splendid book, *Country Remedies*, confirms that the commonest remedy for chilblains was to dip them in the chamber-pot, although wealthy eighteenth-century members of the Harbord family of Lowestoft used wine instead. (Perhaps I should have compromised and gone for dandelion and burdock).

Thrashing chilblains with holly until they bled was a drastic but widespread remedy, while another idea from Essex also involved the use of holly, but this time as an ointment. The berries were powdered and mixed with lard.

Elizabeth Harland's *No Halt At Sunset, The Diary of a Country Housewife*, published in 1951, features this excerpt from a snowbound December when she was asked if there was anything the wretched stuff was good for:

> *Chilblains on the feet. All you have to do is run barefoot in the snow until your feet glow; about five minutes. Have not been plagued with these for years myself, as, in defiance of all the wiseacres, I make a practice of sitting with my feet in the fender whenever possible, and while writing, have them on a hot-water bottle or within scorching distance of an electric fire.*
>
> *'But have more than once applied this drastic-sounding remedy*

with complete success in days gone by. And can still see myself and brother John, having declined to go to a dull party on plea of having bad colds, chasing stocking-and-shoeless up and down the snow-covered tennis lawn on a moonlit January night!

Hidden shallows

A colourful chapter in the history of Norfolk culture has closed with the passing of Henry Kipper in his eighty-sixth year. Henry, alleged father of folk superstar Sid Kipper and erstwhile member of the celebrated Kipper Family, died peacefully in mid-anecdote.

A moving tribute in the *Trunch Trumpet*, official organ of the Sid Kipper Fan Club, emphasises: 'So, in a very real sense, he went quietly in everyone else's sleep.'

Younger son of William and Sarah, he was born on the day the First World War broke out. His father noted in his diary: 'This is the end of civilisation as we know it.' Strangely, he made no mention of the war.

Henry grew up in the little Norfolk village of St Just-near-Trunch where, in 1936, he married Dot Spratt, apparently to the great relief of all, as it meant nobody else would have to marry either of them.

It was in the 1980s that Henry, along with talented son Sid, was discovered by the folk scene. They toured the country, recorded albums and made television and radio appearances.

I interviewed them several times as Henry basked in his reputation for having one of the foremost voices in the country … 'but we don't know who might have the other three'.

Sid went solo in 1991 when the family held a surprise retirement party for Henry. He ran away from the old folkies' home to which he had been sent, and the family lost touch for a few years.

Then, just two weeks before his death, he turned up at the family cottage and, despite the change of locks, managed to gain entrance. There they found him, sitting in his old chair by the fire as if nothing had happened.

The funeral was taken by the vicar of St Just, the Revd 'Call-me-Derek' Bream. He performed a rather modern form of service, which included the coffin being placed in the cloakroom according to the laws of feng shui, and the congregation standing and clapping their hands over their heads as they movingly sang 'Another One Bites the Dust'.

Tributes to Henry have been flooding in, not least from various widows who attended the funeral. A spokesperson for the Erpingham Folk Song and Dance Society said: 'As a singer, his refusal to be tied down to the well-tempered scale was challenging.'

Cromer's Folk on the Pier organisers opined: 'We will never see his like again. But rest assured that if we do, we'll run 'em out of town.'

Dunspreddin's warning

A recent letter to the *Eastern Daily Press* proposed the building of a substantial new town to meet Norfolk's housing needs and to save the county's character.

The 'obvious location' was in the middle, providing all necessary development land for decades and thus preventing the rest of Norfolk being destroyed by urban sprawl.

A bold vision on the face of it, a radical solution to soothe expansionists and drawbridge supporters alike.

But even the best-laid schemes can go slightly awry...

Blessed with a foresight not afforded to landowners, developers, planners and councillors, I have studied a report in the *EDP* for 15 May, 2052. It makes doubtful reading:

Last night's meeting of Upper Dunspreddin Town Council was marked by anxious calls to preserve the area's traditional qualities. Chairman Edgar Runcton-Holme warned that the town was in serious danger of finishing up just like everywhere else in Norfolk – empty shops in the centre, bunged up with traffic and lacking enough wind turbines to generate power for a growing population.

He demanded urgent talks with his opposite numbers in Lower Dunspreddin, Dunspreddin Tofts, Dunspreddin Parva, Dunspreddin Bardolph, Dunspreddin Nethergate, Dunspreddin Strawless and Dunspreddin-cum-Pitchfork to revive the campaign for a single-track A47 to and from the Midlands.

'Vice-chairman Alice Guestwick claimed many of the problems were of their own making; the mobile phone museum was in the wrong place next to the drive-through local history centre while the Miniforum didn't look right with yellow curtains and solar panelling.

'Former mayor Charles Lopham proposed more 'adoption' programmes whereby smaller Norfolk communities accepted 'overspill' from the bigger ones.

'He pointed to success stories at Blowyertop (formerly Seething), Stacksville (Bale) and Golikehell (Sloley) as stirring examples.

'Former district nurse Elsie Bedingham said it made sense for the proposed new Norfolk and Norwich Hospital to be sited at Feltwell.

'The meeting concluded with the usual hearty rendering of 'To Be A Farmer's Boy' and community prayers led by the Revd Percy Tibbenham, Rector of St Mawkins's, Dunspreddin-on-the-Sosh.

෨෩

11 *Face to Face*

I have interviewed thousands of interesting folk during a newspaper and radio career stretching back to 1962. It is difficult to draw up a short-list of favourite personalities for there are so many worthy of another nod of gratitude. I'll stay quiet when it comes to the few who not only failed to come up to expectations but also mocked the sort of reputation that singled them out for special attention in the first place. Suffice to hint that the worlds of sport, politics and showbusiness have always harboured members of the awkward squad!

Early days as a newspaper reporter were dominated by retirement presentations, golden weddings and annual dinners. I soon realised the dangers of imbibing too freely before taking down notes, especially when a devoted couple reflecting on fifty years of uninter-rupted bliss insisted on handing round liberal toasts of home-made rhubarb wine. Most supplies, it seemed, had been stored away just after the honeymoon to gather dust and potency for such a golden occasion. Even hardened photographers and battle-scarred senior reporters steered clear of lethal potions until suitable pictures and salient facts had been sorted. Just imagine the pitfalls facing a bottle-scared novice…

A basic flaw in my shorthand technique – I failed to master the art despite years of grim application and a host of sympathetic mentors – meant I often had to put meaningful meat on the driest of bones. At least shortcomings as a note-taker led to my developing a keen sense of listening and a commendable habit of checking care-fully that what I'd written down bore close resemblance to what had been said. Most people were pleased, often flattered, that I took the trouble to inquire. Some even grabbed the chance to make useful amendments before laws of libel came into play.

Of course, I had more licence to thrill on becoming a full-time sports correspondent. Football managers in particular had good reason to be grateful for strict editing of after-match quotes. Most of these bordered on the banal, biased or bewildering – lifeblood of the tabloid troops but unworthy of too much attention in a quality provincial newspaper. I was paid a reasonable wage to deliver my own considered views of a game. I took that role seriously. At least one Norwich City manager suggested I should have been more of an enthusiastic supporter and less of a critical reporter. Of such distinctions are little confrontations made.

A short but glorious career as a showbiz writer seeking scoops along Yarmouth's Golden Mile brought one of the highlights of my working life – an audience with my hero, Eric Morecambe. 'Come in, young man, and take the weight off your notebook,' urged the great comedian as I sidled into the dressing room. Partner Ernie Wise, applying make-up, nodded a greeting and then formed the other half of a crowd scene as Eric held court for over thirty minutes. I didn't get the chance to ask a single question and I couldn't keep up with a torrent of one-liners. I left in a daze, trying to hang on to at least a couple of new gags to impress colleagues back at the office.

I bumped into Eric again seven or eight years later at Carrow Road when I was on Norwich City football reporting duty and Luton Town were the visitors. He asked what I had done with my career since his Yarmouth masterclass during that memorable summer season. I owned up to being a soccer scribe following the fortunes or otherwise of the Canaries. 'You haven't done much, then,' he quipped. I returned the compliment and asked why he was in our fair city. 'I am here, young man, in my proud capacity as a director of Luton Town FC,' he replied. 'Oh,' I countered, 'Well you haven't done much either since we last met.' He chortled, fiddled with his glasses, threatened to deliver one of his famous face-slapping routines and went on his cheery way.

When I exchanged pen for microphone in 1980 as BBC Radio Norfolk went on air, we were given a perfect example to follow at opening time. Terry Wogan presented his entire Radio 2 morning show from our Norfolk Tower studios. I was wheeled in to give the occasion something of an authentic local flavour. My admiration for the Irish wizard of the wireless remains undimmed.

I met and mardled with many other big names from the media and showbiz roundabouts, Alan Whicker, Roy Hudd and Adam Faith among those calling twice. Tommy Steele flew down early to record a lengthy interview before moving on to sign copies of his novel in a Norwich store. Spike Milligan insisted on making the *Dinnertime*

Show a little longer than usual as he played a tune on the chamber pot used for 'pot luck' sessions. Leslie Thomas, one of my favourite writers, proved every bit as chatty, cheerful and charismatic as I wanted him to be. Donald Sinden wrapped those deliciously plum tones around the What's On Diary and Chemists' Rota. His son, Jeremy, followed suit shortly after. Peter Sallis, alias Norman Clegg from *Last of the Summer Wine*, confessed to being very nervous until I recalled his role as Samuel Pepys from the days when television went out live. David Jason woke up on air as our chat started. He had dozed off on arrival from the Norwich Theatre Royal. Irene Handl proved just as delightfully scatty off-stage as she had been on it as Mrs Malaprop in *The Rivals*. Dorothy Tutin was genuinely alarmed at my offer to become Chancellor of the Exchequer when she arrived for a chat on Budget Day.

The cavalcade of home-grown talent was no less formidable or friendly, endearing Norfolk characters glorying in their traditions: Victor Dewing of Briston leading horses through early years of the twentieth century and ploughing the dialect furrows. Roger Goffin of Martham clearing his throat, making the microphone shudder and suggesting 'the old bellows aren't too sharp, boy'. Then, with eyes tight shut, he sang his heart out. Will Baldry of Kirby Cane marking his 100th birthday with a moving rendition of The Farmer's Boy. Former Gorleston lifeboat coxswain George Mobbs recalling epic rescue operations in matter-of-fact tones. Baker and local preacher Jack Gaskin of Hindringham delivering his own Norfolk version of the bread of life. Countless village chroniclers putting their little communities on the map.

Then there were Tuesday tonics dispensed by the incomparable Fred Wigby, dubbed The Grand Old Mardler. He strolled in to talk about anything and everything with relish and humour. I can see him now, crouching at the back of the desk in the studio. The usual microphone had left its fittings as we tried to level it up to a comfortable chatting height. A switch to the other mike brought immediate disaster as it came away in his hand and could not be coaxed back before our live exchange. So, as it dangled, Fred dangled with it. He bobbed up and down on an ocean of chuckles. Suddenly, I could hear him but I couldn't see him. We guffawed through the first minutes of our regular session before an engineer came to restore some sort of order.

Perhaps the most poignant moment of my broadcasting career came when Errol Crossan flew in from Canada for a big reunion of Norwich City's 1958/59 FA Cup side. That was the season when, as a Third

Division club, the Canaries reached the semi-finals, only to lose to Luton 1-0 in a replay. Crossan called to join a clutch of other Carrow Road old boys for a *Dinnertime Show* chat in September, 1984. I played the evocative 'Ballad of Crossan and Bly', written and recorded by my cousin Paul Wyett as a tribute to our Cup heroes. Those twenty-five years melted away as the little winger they called 'Cowboy' when he sported a crewcut and tormented defenders looked straight at me with tears in his eyes. 'I didn't think they would remember me after all this time,' he whispered. I told him they remember all their old friends in Norfolk.

The most unusual interview of my career featured Tom Allen, Lord Nelson's manservant for over a decade. Such contrasting characters from the same small Norfolk village of Burnham Thorpe, their relationship was strained often to the point of breaking down completely. But they mustered enough in common to stay in harness until the great sailor's death at Trafalgar in 1805.

I posed as a naval historian dispatched by the Admiralty to fill in a few missing pieces of Nelson's epic career and tracked Tom Allen down to a rest home for Colourful Bit-Part Players in World History, on the Norfolk coast.

Tom Allen was reluctant at first to discuss his master's personal traits – 'why can't you let his good deeds stand on their own?' – but he gradually warmed to the invitation, albeit with the help of several tankards of frothing ale. He often slipped naturally into a broad Norfolk dialect, maintaining Nelson had encouraged him to do this when they were alone on the high seas.

Here are brief extracts from a three-hour conversation ended by Allen's sudden decision to retire to a hammock strung up in the corner of his room. Loud snores indicated our interview was at an end.

SKIPPER: How did you become Nelson's manservant?

ALLEN: Well, I was bound to know him seeing as how we were both brought up in Burnham Thorpe. I sort of volunteered for the job after he had to get rid of that drunken oaf Frank Lepee. Call that a Norfolk name! Couldn't hold his liquor or his tongue, that one. Horatio had come home to see the family and then it was time for another set-to with the French. He was given the *Agamemnon*, a real beauty with 64 guns, and I know a lot of the crew were Norfolk volunteers. Yes, they liked him no doubt, but anything had to be better than staying around Burnham with all that poverty and misery. Even the parson was struggling!

SKIPPER: This all happened in 1793. But you had no experience of dealing with officers and gentlemen, and your manners, apparently, left much to be desired. Didn't this lead to friction?

ALLEN: Yeh – and I reckon he liked it as much as me! You see, I could say things and do things all these high-ups really wished they could have done. Horatio had to tell me off and, bor, he could let rip now and again – but we allus knew where we stood, Norfolk men don't go in for all this lardy-dardy talk. What was it I said to Horatio one night when he was being a right old misery? 'Don't care what faces you pull or how many moods you go through, old partner, I'd still give an arm and a leg to see you alone with the gal Emma…'

SKIPPER: Very amusing, but you tested his patience so often that he branded you an illiterate beast and a notorious liar in front of others and threatened to get rid of you many times. What was it he said after you lost a case containing all his papers and £200? 'He will one day ruin me by his ignorance, obstinacy and lies.'

ALLEN: I might have guessed you'd pick that one out – so have this in return: 'He is faithful and attached, with great shrewdness mixed with his simplicity.' But look here, all these fancy words don't alter the fact I was with him for over ten years. We had our ups and downs, quite nasty some of 'em, but I never felt he would push me out. Blarst, I was too useful. I understood him better than anyone, and he could be an awkward customer, y'know. When he had to have his right arm off he started moaning about being a burden to his friends and useless to his country. I soon put him straight and told him left-handed admirals from Norfolk could still do their job properly. I even fixed him up a contraption of pulley and cord so he could call for help if he needed it in the middle of the night.

SKIPPER: Weren't you rude about Nelson's drinking habits?

ALLEN: No – I was just being helpful. He couldn't take very much and I could always tell the danger signs, especially when he was on the champagne. I told him he'd be ill if he didn't stop, and he knew I was right. Once I had to lead him from the table after five glasses of wine, and he took my advice so that didn't happen again. Just the same when he forgot his cloak on deck on a wet old night and went and caught the shivers. When a junior rating had tried to point out the dangers rather timidly he laughed, 'My anxiety for my country will keep me warm and dry.' Then I had a go at him. He looked sheepish, turned smartly and fetched his cloak from the cabin.

SKIPPER: Weren't you accused of being disrespectful towards Nelson and many influential people he met and dealt with?

ALLEN: Hundreds of times! But like I said before, the master and me understood each other, even if he had to put on a bit of a show when them big-wigs were about. Who was that chap who became King of the Two Sicilies when old Napoleon got sorted out? You know, Ferdinand the Fourth. Well, when I got to shake hands with him at a posh do I just said, 'How do you do, Mr King!' – and Horatio had a rare job not to laugh out loud. You should have heard what he called Mr King after he'd gone!

SKIPPER: Did Nelson have a Norfolk accent?

ALLEN: Oh, there were definite bits of Norfolk in his talk when he was with me and other men from home. You couldn't spend all that time in the Burnhams without picking up traces, though he could get a bit upper-crust when he liked. When he used to swear at me and get all agitated, a few good old Norfolk expressions came out. And he'd go a bit red when I saluted and smiled in appreciation! Like all great leaders, he could get on with all classes and all sorts – and there wouldn't ha'been much point talking a lot of squit to that Ferdinand bloke.

SKIPPER: How did you react to Nelson's death?

ALLEN: Blubbered like a wench for days on end. Couldn't believe it. I was working ashore when news came from the *Victory* that we had won at Trafalgar but lost the greatest man Norfolk ever produced. I know my master would have survived if I'd been there to look after him...

SKIPPER: How will Nelson be remembered?

ALLEN: Well, he had his faults. Too weak with women and too vain for a start. But as a brave and talented commander he will always be miles out in front. Horatio inspired people from all walks of life and his death really was a national calamity. How did the poet Robert Southery put it? 'Men started at the intelligence and turned pale as if they had heard of the loss of a dear friend.' That's exactly how it did hit us. Now I must leave it there. The *Agamemnon* sails at dawn and I must rest before I join my master and the Mediterranean fleet. Please God, us lads from Burnham Thorpe will always do our duty…

12 *A Fatal Duel*

Norfolk's reputation for solving most disputes by means of vigorous but fair-minded debate has suffered one or two nasty jolts over the centuries. One such diversion arrived on 20 August 1698, when two Norfolk worthies crossed swords for the most famous duel in local history.

It all began with rumours of name-calling. It ended with one protagonist fatally wounded and the other forced to flee as a fugitive. On the 300th anniversary of this bizarre episode I looked for a few fresh clues leading up to this deadly event...

Sir Henry Hobart of Blickling Hall was feeling decidedly sorry for himself. He had lost an important election and a small fortune to boot, being forced to sell of some of the family estates to pay his backers.

Angry and humiliated at rejection by Norfolk's voters, the Whig grandee who had been knighted as a boy of thirteen when Charles II dined at Blickling sat brooding over his misfortunes.

Loss of influence and of parliamentary privilege were bound to hurt one of the area's leading personalities. Then came insult to add to all the indignities – and the quick-tempered Sir Henry yielded to rage and resentment with fatal consequences.

It is not known who brought the tittle-tattle to his country seat, whether it was passed on with relish or foreboding or where it might have originated. Clearly, the master of Blickling was caught on the raw and arrogantly refused to treat these rumours as no more than mud-stirring in the wake of political intrigue.

Sir Henry's highly sensitive state was made for drama. As he growled and prowled beneath the turrets and gables of his palatial home near Aylsham, he cursed that upstart squire of Great Witchingham Hall. He would have satisfaction!

Oliver Le Neve was supposed to be spreading stories about his illustrious neighbour to the effect that Hobart had lost the Norfolk election through an act of cowardice in Ireland. Hobart had been alongside King William on his victorious campaign as a Gentleman of the Horse, their exploits including the Battle of the Boyne.

What was the alleged cowardly act being touted? Why did it take so long for any malicious gossip, whatever its source or veracity, to surface from that episode of 1690? Why should Le Neve make such accusations? Why did Hobart refuse to make any concessions to the rumour machine despite Le Neve' strong protestations of innocence?

There was no history of animosity between the two men, although their political differences were obvious. The Norfolk country squire of traditional Tory views held no brief for King William and his courtiers, and probably took some satisfaction from Hobart's humbling at the hustings. But he had no reason to openly quarrel with his formidable neighbour.

Le Neve's personal circumstances at the time suggested he wanted a quiet life. He had just married his second wife, having been left a widower two years earlier, and was looking forward to a period of gentle readjustment with his new spouse, his son and three small daughters.

He was fond of gardening and hunting, on friendly terms with other squires in the district and a diligent observer of all formalities in his administrative work. He was a justice of the peace, a captain of militia and a commissioner of taxes.

In short, Le Neve was a respectable pillar of Norfolk society, the last man you would expect to be hurtled into the murky world of scurrilous insults, angry challenges and deadly duels.

When Hobart's challenge arrived, the amiable squire of Great Witchingham Hall probably first thought it a poor joke or a simple mistake. He wrote immediately to deny he had ever uttered the words attributed to him, and pledged to find out who was spreading such dark mischief. Headstrong Hobart would have none of it.

He stormed over to Reepham and publicly repeated his accusation against Le Neve, adding for good measure that the squire of Witchingham had penned his letter of denial because he was too scared to fight.

Le Neve had no option. He accepted the challenge in a letter that underlined his courage and humility. This could not have been written by anyone other than a person of high principles:

Honored Sr,
I am very sorry I was not at Reifham yesterday, when you gave your-
self the trouble of appearing there, that I might not only have further

*justified the Truth of my not saying what is reported I did, but that I
might have told you that I wrote not that letter to avoid fighting you;
but that, if the credit of yor author has confirmd you in the belief of it,
I am ready & desirous to meet you when & where you please to assign.
If otherwise, I expect your Author's name in return to this, that I may
take my satisfaction there, or else conclude the Imputacion sprung
from Blickling & send you time & place; for the matter shall not rest
as it is, tho' it cost the life of*

Yor Servt,
OLIVER NEVE

Le Neve obviously thought his number was up. He knew Hobart was
a top-class swordsman while he was a rather clumsy performer – and
left-handed as well. They met on Saturday, 20 August 1698, amid the
bracken and heather of Cawston Heath, the selected spot about
halfway between their respective homes.

We must assume there were seconds and other spectators, all of
them resigned to a straightforward victory for the Blickling man, tall
and erect, over his short, plain opponent. It looked ever more of a
formality when Hobart wounded Le Neve in the arm.

Le Neve, perhaps in a burst of desperation, lunged forward to
run his sword deep into Hobart's stomach. It was the decisive blow.
The crumpled baronet was carried back to Blickling where he died
next day.

The unexpected collector of the victor's laurels on Cawston Heath
soon realised he was liable to conviction for the murder of a man
he had never wished to harm. Some reward for acting with integrity
and honour and accepting the challenge forced upon him! Now
the Hobart family, a grieving widow to the fore, were thirsting
for revenge.

They had powerful court and parliamentary connections. Le Neve
fled to Holland, a price on his head, but eventually returned to stand
trial. With much public sympathy in his favour, he was acquitted of
any blame, but life after the hearing was crammed with misfortunes.
His second wife died in 1704. Le Neve married Elizabeth Sheffield in
1707, but she died three months later. The grief-stricken squire of
Great Witchingham died in 1711 only a few months after the death of
his only son.

Oliver Le Neve was forty-eight. All the evidence suggests he had
been drawn into one of the most bizarre episodes in Norfolk history
by spiteful gossip and innuendo.

Three hundred years after that fateful confrontation on Cawston Heath it remains difficult to feel much sympathy for the character who provoked it and perished as a result.

Weighed down by electoral defeat and mounting debts, Hobart took on the role of blustering bully of Blickling. He met his comeuppance at the unlikely hands of the reluctant warrior of Witchingham.

The 300th anniversary offered a pertinent reminder that old-fashioned virtues can carry the day - even if vindication carries a cruel cost.

Family backgrounds

The Hobarts were well established at Blickling Hall by the time Sir Henry followed in his father's political footsteps. He sat for King's Lynn in the last of Charles II's parliaments and when his father, Sir John Hobart, died in 1683, Henry was regarded as leader of the Country Party in Norfolk.

He represented the county in the Convention Parliament of 1689, was defeated in the election of the following year when a Tory majority was returned, but was victorious again when the Whigs came back to power in 1695. Another election took place in the summer of 1698. Although it did not substantially alter the balance of parties, Sir Henry was one of the established Whig members to fall.

He was married to Elizabeth, elder daughter and co-heiress of Joseph Maynard. Their only son, John, later to become Earl of Buckinghamshire, was only five when his father died following the duel on Cawston Heath. Six daughters survived their father. One of them, Henrietta, afterwards Countess of Suffolk, became notorious as the mistress of George II.

᛭

Oliver Le Neve came from an old Norfolk family who combined successful business in London with ownership of landed property in their home county. Inheriting his wealth from a rich uncle who made his name as a stationer, Le Neve settled at Great Witchingham Hall in 1692.

He married Anne, only daughter of Sir John Gawdy of West Harling, by whom he had a son and three daughters. His political sympathies were with the Tory and High Church party.

During Le Neve's exile in Holland following his duel with Hobart, supporters kept him fully informed of all moves in their campaign on his behalf. There was a regular exchange of presents, artichokes and Norfolk ale among the items making their way to Le Neve.

In return, Giles Bladwell of Swannington begged him to buy Mrs Bladwell a dozen fine Holland shifts, and in selecting them to 'remember she is of the fat size'.

Great Witchingham Hall, now the home of turkey tycoon Bernard Matthews, was largely rebuilt in the Elizabethan style in the 1870s.

Crumbling monument

The Duel Stone, a mile east of the village of Cawston, marks the dramatic meeting of 1698.

A mixture of twittering birds and roaring traffic greeted my anniversary visit to this site only a matter of yards from the Woodrow Garage on the busy B1149 Norwich–Holt road. A plaque on the gate uncomfortably close to the highway summarised the story behind a short pillar surmounted by a pumpkin-like urn: revealing that the monument and surrounding land had been given to the National Trust in 1964.

Iron railings, square and forbidding, surrounded the shingled plot flanked by trees and bushes. A cornfield ripening beyond and blackberries promising an autumn bounty nearby provided welcome signs of colour and life in this funereal setting.

The monument was erected in 1770 by Wiggett Bulwer of Wood Dalling. The initials H.H. cut into the memorial remain a discernible tribute to Henry Hobart, fatally wounded near this spot when it was wild heathland rather than a little bit of history just a few paces from a bustling road.

The house next door to the garage was the Woodrow Inn until it closed in 1964. The pub, naturally, made plenty of the nearby memorial, and in the smoke-room was a framed portrait of Sir Henry Hobart with a short biographical sketch and a reference to the duel beneath.

Nowadays, the bulk of folk flashing past or filling up with petrol at the garage are oblivious to the fact they are travelling along Norfolk's very first 'Duel carriageway'.

Traffic's snarl drowns out birdsong's lament over a fascinating Norfolk monument.

13 A Parson Phase

One of my favourite characters from the pages of Norfolk history is a genial country rector who kept a diary of the commonplace, destined to become part of our rich inheritance.

Parson James Woodforde of Weston Longville maintained his unique record for forty-three years, with the final entry on Sunday 17 October 1802. He died on New Year's Day, 1803.

As a devout diary-keeper myself, with comprehensive daily gleanings since 1984, I reflected on the enduring appeal of his musings two centuries after his death. For someone supposed to be interested in little more than tables groaning with rich food, he dealt with a remarkably wide social menu...

A stroll round the good parson's parish, straining to keep a toe-hold on the countryside a few miles north-west of Norwich, could hardly qualify as a tour of celebration.

Heavy traffic thunders through to drown birdsong, shake hedges and put pedestrians on full alert. There's part of the Bernard Matthews turkey empire on the old aerodrome to one side, and the dinosaur park tourist attraction on the other. The liveliest imagination is hard pushed to guess what an eighteenth-century cleric would make of it all.

Even so, the still, small voice of thanksgiving can yet be heard by taking refuge in the splendidly spacious All Saints' Church, the welcoming Parson Woodforde pub opposite and a host of attractive houses that wouldn't look out of place on a calendar extolling the delights of rural retirement.

Pointing the way to fascinating pages of social history is a village sign presented by veterans of the 466th Bomb Group, USAAF, in memory of colleagues who died while stationed here during the last war. Coats of arms on the sign include that of New College, Oxford, where James Woodforde was educated and ordained as a deacon. The college has been a landowner in the parish since the beginning of the fourteenth century and is still patron of the benefice.

Born at Ansford in Somerset in June, 1740, James Woodforde was baptised three days later, being very ill', by his father, the Rector of Ansford and Vicar of Castle Cary. Young James recovered and flourished to be elected a scholar at Winchester College before moving on to Oxford. He held a number of curacies in his native Somerset as a prelude to being appointed in 1774 to the living of Weston Longville. He didn't take up the post until May, 1776.

His diary, kept from the age of eighteen until a few weeks before his death on New Year's Day in 1803, is a mine of information about the lives of ordinary people in the second half of the eighteenth century – farmers, shopkeepers, attorneys, servants, squires, doctors, blacksmiths and merchants. While great events such as the emergence of America and the French Revolution were unfolding in the wider world beyond, the diary records the thoughts and deeds of the amiable parson as he busies himself with the matters of Norfolk village life.

A sociable bachelor, he was looked after by his niece Nancy along with five servants, and constantly showed a reverence for small events and the domestic odds and ends of existence. The diary is also a meticulously kept account book, with the price of food, stagecoaches, household necessities, theatres and medicines all carefully noted.

Although Parson Woodforde never married, he did propose to a Miss Betsy White of Shepton Mallet in 1774, but she jilted him later for a rich Mr Webster of Devonshire, whom she married a year later. Our Norfolk Bachelor of Divinity was not averse to a spot of flirting, and he recounts taking off a young widow's garter and good-naturedly exchanging a pair of his garters for a pair of hers.

It is this spirited, almost earthy, side of his character that endears him to so many through pages that sparkle now as brightly as the waters of the Wensum where he landed pike and trout over two centuries ago. Woodforde lived in his living, looking after parishioners himself instead of making do with an underpaid curate. He bought gin and cognac from smugglers, lapped up good food washed down with port and Madeira and gambled regularly at cards, albeit for small stakes. An impish sense of fun shines through many incidents recorded in the diary, not least New Year celebrations... 'Nancy and Betsie Davie locked me in the great parlour, and both fell on me and pulled my wig almost to pieces – I paid them for it however.'

For those who seek it, there is plenty of evidence to show the Church generally in the doldrums during this era. Parson Woodforde disapproved strongly of singing in church and anything which went beyond formal Christian duties regulating society. 'I read Prayers and Preached this Afternoon at Weston' seems to sum up his weekly labours, and he was irritated if other calls came his way. Many ceremonies, including christenings, were carried out in his parlour, and his church filled only for thanksgivings for military victories and recoveries from illness of members of the royal family.

He says so much about meals that a reputation for gluttony has grown over the years. Some enthusiasts, however, claim he should be indicted merely for conviviality. He relished agreeable company, and food simply paved the way to some intimacy and pleasure in what was a rather lonely existence. It is also worth recalling the old custom of cramming the table with many dishes of roast, game and fish instead of serving them as separate courses. He extended those pleasures involved by including the day's menus in his diary – even in the last words written in October, 1802: 'Very weak this Morning, scarce able to put on my Clothes and with great difficulty, get down Stairs with help … Dinner to day, Rost Beef etc.'

Perhaps the sharp contrast between the parson's tidy portion and meagre rations handed out to the majority of people around him has fed that reputation for greed. Certainly, he took a pragmatic view of hardship, as is evidenced by an entry like this:

> We dined at 3 o'clock, and after we had smoked a Pipe etc, we took a ride to the House of Industry about 2 miles West of Dereham … About 380 Poor in it now, but they don't look either healthy or cheerful, a great Number die there, 27 have died since Christmas last (in three months). We returned from there to the King's Arms, and there we supped and spent the evening together.

In fact, Woodforde did appreciate the comparative comfort in which he lived on about £400 a year, and he showed regular charity towards itinerants who called at the rectory. He didn't ask for fees for marriages or burials, and when local farmers brought him their annual tithes, it descended rapidly into a 'frolic' full of beer and bonhomie.

Such a generous nature is enshrined in the memorial tablet on the chancel wall in Weston Longville Church, just above a diamond-shaped tile indicating his burial place. The tablet was erected by his nephew Bill and faithful niece Nancy:

> His parishioners held him in the highest esteem and veneration and as

a tribute to his memory followed him to the grave. The poor feel a severe loss as they were the constant objects of his bounty.

It was shortly after the First World War that a Hertfordshire doctor persuaded John Beresford to take a look at a diary kept by an ancestor who had been the rector of a small village near Norwich. Beresford was captivated, and in 1924 published the first of his five-volume extract of the diary. Its popularity since has been equalled only by that other and markedly different cleric masterpiece, *Kilvert's Diary*, published a decade later.

James Woodforde referred to his musings as a 'trifling' book, and could have nursed no ambitions to see it emerge as one of the most telling chronicles of the Georgian age. The work of an ordinary man is now accepted as extraordinary for the insight it gives to domestic and social life in the last four decades of the eighteenth century.

Just as significantly, it is highly entertaining. Noisy toads, drunken pigs, pregnant maids, nuisance woodpeckers, strange dreams, November primroses, June tempests, cruel winters, fainting fits … and countless other topics demanding attention, long before turkeys and dinosaurs came on the Weston Longville scene.

Favourite entries from *A Country Parson's Diary*

June 4, 1776 *My tooth pained me all night, got up a little after 5 this morning, & sent for one Reeves, a man who draws teeth in this parish, and about 7 he came and drew my tooth, but shockingly bad indeed, he broke away a great piece of my gum and broke one of the fangs of the tooth, it gave me exquisite pain all the day after, and my Face was swelled prodigiously in the evening and much pain. Very bad and in much pain the whole day long. Gave the old man that drew it however 0.2.6. He is too old, I think, to draw teeth, can't see very well.*

February 14, 1777 *To 36 children being Valentine's day and what is customary for them to go about in these parts, this day gave 0.3.0 being one penny apiece to each of them.*

March 29, 1777 *Andrews the Smuggler brought me this night about 11 o'clock a bagg of Hyson Tea 6 pd weight. He frightened us a little by whistling under the Parlour window just as we were going to bed. I gave him some Geneva and paid him for the tea at 10/6 per pd.*

June 4, 1777 *The toads in my great Pond made an extraordinary loud noise for this last week past. This being his Majesty's Birth Day had my Blunderbuss fired of by Bill above 2 hands high three times in honour of the day, and with powder only.*

April 15, 1778 *Brewed a vessell of strong Beer today. My two large Piggs, by drinking some Beer grounds taking out of one of my Barrels today got so amazingly drunk by it, that they were not able to stand and appeared like dead things almost, and so remained all night from dinner time today. I never saw Piggs so drunk in my life. I slit their ears for them without feeling.*

April 16, 1778 *My 2 Piggs are still unable to walk yet, but they are better than they were yesterday. They tumble about the yard and can by no means stand at all steady yet. In the afternoon my 2 Piggs were tolerably sober.*

November 21, 1778 *I told my Maid Betty this morning that the other maid Nanny looked so big about the Waist that I was afraid she was with Child, but Betty told me she thought not, but would soon inform me if it is so.*

January 31, 1780 *A very comical dull day with us all. Sister Clarke very low. In the evening Sam spoke in favour of the Methodists rather too much I think. We did not play cards this evening as usual.*

July 24, 1781 *I read a good deal of the History of England today to Nancy whilst she was netting her Apron. Very dry again. I feed my Geese with Cabbage now.*

January 26, 1784 *I rejoiced much this morning on shooting an old woodpecker, which had teized me a long Time in pulling out the Reed from my House.*

September 22, 1785 *Mr Custance sent us a Brace of Partridges this Morn which was very kind of him – Mr Micklethwaite has not sent us any, tho' daily out with a Double-barrelled Gun and often in my Closes close to my House.*

December 29, 1786 *Had another Tub of Gin and another of the best Coniac Brandy brought me this Evening ab' 9. We heard a thump at* *the Front Door about that time, but did not know what it was till I went out and found the 2 Tubs – but nobody there.*

March 11, 1791 *The Stiony on my right Eye-lid still swelled and inflamed very much. As it is commonly said that the Eye-lid being rubbed by the tail of a black Cat would do it much good if not entirely cure it, and having a black Cat, a little before dinner I made a trial of it, and very soon after dinner I found my Eye-lid much abated of the swelling and almost free from Pain.*

October 12, 1792 *John Buck, the blacksmith, who was lately informed against for having a Tub of Gin found in his House that was smuggled, by two Excise Officers, was pretty easy fined. Dinner to day boiled Tongue and Turnips and a fine Couple of Ducks rosted.*

December 28, 1798 *Frost last Night & this morning & all the Day intense – it froze in every part of the House even in the Kitchen. Milk & Cream tho' kept in the Kitchen all froze. Meat like blocks of Wood. It froze in the Kitchen even by the fire in a very few Minutes. So severe Weather I think I never felt before.*

☙

14 Christmas Past

Christmas can be a time of overblown expectations. 'Nothing like it used to be,' we mutter as another expensive festive fling shrivels away like a limp balloon behind the trimmings. 'They have far too much,' is the predictable left-over tossed towards youngsters playing in a cardboard box up the corner. 'Anyone interested in tea?' comes across as an accusation while sales bargains and sunshine brochures dance across the television screen.

We close our eyes to seek consolation in a time when Christmas really was a season of peace and goodwill, of joyful family reunions round an open fire and spontaneous storytelling. A little healthy nostalgia should not do any harm, although we can become obsessed with the idea that every Christmas past was so much better than an over-commercialised, underwhelming Christmas present.

There's a strong tendency to indulge more in a journey of imagination than to settle for a record of fact. Perhaps a quiet stroll along the Norfolk bookshelves can combine the two in a way that satisfies yearnings for yesterday while accepting a few blessings of today.

My seasonal saunter across the centuries begins with the comforting sight of one of Norfolk's most formidable medieval housewives sorting out her Christmas programme. Margaret Paston wrote many of the celebrated family letters destined to open a window on the world of the fifteenth century during one of the most turbulent periods in English history. The festivities of 1459 were put on hold after the death of Sir John Fastolf, an important and influential friend of the family who gave Caister Castle as his home address.

With her husband John in London, Margaret Paston took advice on proper etiquette from the doyenne of Norfolk ladies, Lady Morley. A period of mourning was demanded, but the household was also anxious to make merry. This is what Margaret wrote to her husband:

Please you to know that I sent your eldest son to my Lady Morley to have knowledge what sports were used at her house at Christmas next following after the decease of my Lord, her husband. And she said that there were no disguisings nor harping, luting or singing, nor any lewd sports, but just playing at the tables and chess and cards. Such sports she gave folk leave to play and no others.

So, charades and choruses were out but Newmarket and nap could form part of the festive activities in the big Paston household of 1459. No doubt, there were several courses for the festive feast, including old favourites boiled chicken, roast pork, goose or game and baked meats and custards.

By the time Daniel Defoe came this way in 1724, on a *Tour Through the Whole Island of Great Britain*, turkeys were prominent on a festive menu. He reported on Christmas dinners that walked to London as turkeys and geese from Norfolk and Suffolk were driven to the capital on foot:

A prodigious number are brought up to London in droves from the farthest parts of Norfolk, even from the fen country about Lynn, Downham, Wisbech and the Washes, as also from all the east side of Norfolk and Suffolk of whom it is very frequent now to meet drovers with a thousand, sometimes two thousand in a drove. Besides these methods of driving the creatures on foot, they have of late, also invented a new method of carriage, being carts formed on purpose with four stories a stage to put the creatures in one above the other.

A century later, when radical William Cobbett included Norfolk in his tours of the English countryside on horseback – his famous *Rural Rides* – our highways won more plaudits than they collect from most travellers today, feathered or otherwise. Cobbett set out from London at the end of October in 1821, reaching Norfolk in early December. He left full of admiration and respect 'for this county of excellent farmers and hearty, open and spirited men'. His Christmas Eve chronicle continued:

The Norfolk people are quick and smart in their motions and in their speaking. Very neat and trim in all their farming concerns and very skilful. Their land is good, their roads are level, and the bottom of their soil is dry, to be sure; these are great advantages, but they are diligent and make the most of everything.

Not bad for a tucked-away place on the road to nowhere.

Of course, our clergy are exceptionally busy at this time of the year. Luckily for us, two outstanding men of the cloth found time to light up the pages of Norfolk history with plenty of Christmas entries in their diaries.

Parson James Woodforde had the living at Weston Longville near Norwich from 1776 until his death on New Year's Day in 1803. His first Christmas in Norfolk was marked by a shilling apiece and a good meal for the poor of the parish:

> *By God's blessing I intend doing the same next Christmas Day. Gave old Richard Bates an old black coat and waistcoat. I had a fine sirloin of beef roasted and plumb puddings. It was very dark at church this aft. I could scarce see…*

> **December 31, 1780** *This being the last day of the year we sat up until after 12 o'clock, then drank a happy new year to all our friends and went to bed. We were very merry indeed after supper till 12. Nancy and Betsie Davie locked me into the great parlour, and both fell on me and pulled my wig about to pieces. I paid them for it, however."*

> **December 25, 1791** *this being Christmas I walked to church this morning and read prayers and administered the Holy Sacrament to 22 communicants. Gave for an offering at the altar two shillings and six-pence. None from Weston House at church this morn, the weather being very cold, wet and windy, and extreme bad walking, being all ice underfoot. My foot extremely painful, hard matter to get to and from church, but thank God, I went through it all better than I expected.*

> **Christmas Day, 1794** *It was very cold indeed this morning, and the snow in many places quite deep with an east wind. About 11 this morning, I walked to church and read prayers and administered the Holy Sacrament. Had but few communicants the weather so bad. Immediately after the morning service so far as before the administration of the Holy Sacrament I was attacked with an epileptic fit, and fainted away in my desk, but Thank God! soon recovered and went through the remaining part of my duty.*

> **December 26** *Thank God! Had a pretty good night last night, and I hope am something better, but rather languid and low. Could eat but very little for dinner today of calves fry and rabbit roasted. I drank*

*plentifully of port wine after dinner, instead of one glass, drank
seven or eight wineglasses and it seemed to do me much good, being
better for it.*

It seemed there were fewer festive fun and games for the Revd
Benjamin Armstrong, Vicar of East Dereham from 1850 to 1888, and
another wonderful Norfolk diary keeper. His Christmas Day report
for 1862 carried an abrupt edge:

*A hard day, as I was single-handed. There were weddings, services,
morning (100 communicants), afternoon and evening and finally a
funeral.*

Christmas Day, 1874 *The thermometer being 15 degrees below
freezing point, many were kept away from church through the cold.
Several sudden deaths owing to the severity of the weather. The bell
tolls every day in the fog.*

December 27, 1880 *What a year this has been! Frightful colliery
explosions, railway accidents, shipwrecks, the war broken out again at
the Cape, Ireland on the edge of rebellion and two English clergymen
in jail, reminding one more of the Elizabethan than the Victorian age.*

Christmas Day 1885 *One of my curates had such a frightful cold
that he could do very little in the way of duty. Then our unamiable
organist played atrociously at service, and would have played the
Easter Anthem had he not been corrected by one of the senior members of the choir. Then the attenuated choir had but very little voice
from singing carols in the cold night air.*

Henry Rider Haggard and daughter Lilias formed one of the most
prolific family forces in Norfolk literary history. Of course, Henry had
peered down *King Solomon's Mines* and listened to *She Who Must Be
Obeyed* before he became a gentleman farmer in his native county. In
1898 he compiled *A Farmer's Year* as he worked the land at Bedingham
and Ditchingham. This is part of his Christmas Day record:

*The frost broke yesterday, with the result that this Christmas has not
the beauty of that of last year, the weather being dull and mild,
towards nightfall softening into rain. In the afternoon I went to hear
some carol singing in the neighbouring church of Broome.*

Afterwards a friend of mine, who lives there, gave me some curious facts, illustrative of the decrease of population of that parish. It is his habit to make a present of meat at Christmas to every cottage inhabitant of Broome, and he informed me that the difference in its cost owing to the shrinkage of population between this year and last is something really remarkable.

The drift from the land underlined crises in the farming industry, and there could be no hiding from grim realities, even on Christmas Day.

On Christmas Eve, 1939, as the country waited for the unfettered dragons of war to breathe fire, Lilias Rider Haggard wrote this poignant passage in her *Norfolk Notebook*:

The other day I was in Norwich market and stopped to watch people buying bunches of berried holly and little Christmas trees from a stall. It was a dismal afternoon, the skies were grey, and a biting wind crept round the corner and nipped the end of one's nose, but the buyers chose their holly and trees and mostly went off with a cheery word and a smile.

'Well,' said a stout and homely housewife, tucking her awkward and prickly burden under her arm, 'There's only one child at home this Christmas, and the Lord knows when I'll get the others back again, but I sez to the old man, "We'll have the tree and all, and if there's not much to hang on it, we'll have to do with hope for a trimmin'. They'll like to think of us just as usual."'

Michael Home's Breckland books included *Autumn Fields*, first published in 1944. He denied it was an autobiography, describing it instead as the history of a small and remote community 'of which I was part and of whose lives and doings I have constituted myself the narrator and interpreter.' He recalled the build-up to Christmas in a Breckland village:

Years later, when I was at home, I would lie awake in my bed to hear the carol singers. Each individual halt could be judged for the sound of the singing would come clear across the fields and through the frosty night. Then it would move on, and it was when the sound came from the near distance and then slowly receded that it would make a kind of lullaby, and at once I would be asleep. By then it would be Christmas Day, and it was on a Christmas Day that I was born.

Fenland writer Edward Storey was brought up in the decade before the Second World War, his world balanced precariously between agriculture and the brick industry. His autobiography, *Fen Boy First*, published in 1992, included this Christmas drama:

> *One year the decorations caught fire from one of the Chinese lanterns and all the balloons burst. There was a great fanning of arms and towels and stamping of feet. The room filled with a grey cloud of smoke that spread into a black snowstorm. I rushed out into the yard shouting Fire! Fire! but there was no-one to hear me… When Mother called me back into the house, the panic was over. The smoke was disappearing through the open window and I could see quite clearly the unperturbed faces of the china dogs on the mantelpiece.*

Norfolk comedian Sidney Grapes of Potter Heigham contributed his wonderful Boy John letters to the *Eastern Daily Press* from 1946 until his death in 1958. One of the earliest letters was printed on Christmas Eve in 1946. After extending season's greetings, the Boy John highlighted Granfar's disillusionment with the postwar world:

> *He mob about everything nowadays. He go down the pub every night, he come back a'mobbin' about the beer, he say he's right glad when he're had enough of it.*

Perhaps the Boy John's most famous seasonal offering came one year a few weeks before Christmas. He put this notice on his garage window at Potter Heigham where he plied his trade in the motor industry:

> *A happy Christmas to all my customers what have paid their bills and a prosperous New Year to them what hent!*

Finally, a Norfolk country housewife takes centre stage. Elizabeth Harland's book *No Halt At Sunset* was first published in 1951 full of rural delights, recipes and all topics to the fore just after the war – including rationing. Her Christmas Day entry put the timeless message of joyful giving in a homely setting:

> *Years ago I was told of an elderly couple who literally hadn't a penny to spare, but each spring the old man hunted the fields for plovers' eggs and brought them as a gift to his wife. When he died a neighbour*

remembered, and sought some for the widow, only to learn that she'd always loathed the things.
'But your husband always gave them to you!"
'Yes, but you see, he had nothing else to give, so I let him think I loved them.'

๑๑

15 Last of a Line

Eric Edwards doesn't go a bundle on modern methods while he works in water up to his knees.

He is one of the last hand-working reed cutters in Norfolk, and his ruddy-faced smile cannot disguise sadness at presiding over the end of an era. Man must soon yield completely to the machine.

Eric has been employed by the Broads Authority since 1967 to manage reed beds and grazing marshes, the scythe an essential tool in his world still rubbing shoulders with Victorian times:

> *The old boys who taught me to handle one of these were true craftsmen as they cut the reeds for thatching. Now it really looks like the end of the line. I did train a couple of lads but they moved on to other things. You can't learn this from a book, but only from being on the marsh.*

I first met Eric forty years ago when he was a hard-tackling player on the local football scene and I was a cub reporter on the touchline. He brings the same brand of enthusiasm and commitment to his role of Broadland buccaneer at How Hill nature reserve by the River Ant at Ludham.

Eric admits mowing is exacting graft and he has to put up with plenty of ribbing about living in the past. But heavy machinery, based on power cutters designed for harvesting rice in the Far East, can damage the reed root systems and make deep ridges in the soil. A small cutter with a box is the better way to complement hand scything. 'The How Hill reed beds have never looked better. They are thriving on good management.'

Over 5000 bundles of reed are cut on his patch each year, most of them going to local thatchers. A bundle costs about £1.85. The earliest reed cutters, fishermen of the nineteenth century, sold them at just over a shilling a fathom. Five or six bundles made up a fathom.

Norfolk reed is a durable, high-quality thatching material. A well-thatched roof should last about fifty years, is naturally energy-efficient and enhances rural locations. The reed-cutting industry benefits both reed and wildlife by harvesting in alternate winters, safeguarding areas that if neglected would disappear under encroaching scrub and young trees.

Although there has been some concern that the quality of reed in East Anglia has declined owing to poor water quality, national research has shown that this is unfounded. Good reed depends primarily on good reed bed management.

Before answering Eric's call to join him on a cutting safari, I consulted the apprentices' handbook, written just over a century ago by Ernest Suffling. This description in *The Land of the Broads* might easily have been penned on the morning I tried my hand at one of Broadland's oldest crafts:

> *During any open weather that may occur after Christmas, reed cutting is commenced and continued until the work is completed in the early spring. It is, in fact, carried on until the sap begins to rise and the young shoots are just appearing.*
>
> *The cutting is done either by men, who wear large waterproof boots, standing in the water or from flat-bottomed punts or reed-boats. A plank is used, which either projects over the bow of the boat, or is laid flat on the stumps of the cut reeds which easily supports the weight of a man.*
>
> *In cutting, an upward stroke is made with the sickle (the reed being held in bunches by the left hand), and care is taken to cut the reed as far below water as possible, as a saying prevails that an inch of reed below water is worth two above it. This may be accounted for from the fact that the green part below the water turns, when dry, to a rusty black, becomes as hard as horn, and is consequently much more durable when placed upon the roof of a house in the form of thatch, with only these hard 'butts', exposed to the weather.*
>
> *When the boat is properly loaded it is propelled by a long pole called a quant to a landing place - or, as it is here called, staithe and the reed carefully landed.*

Eric showed me how to hold the scythe against a backcloth that could have been prepared by Constable or Turner. A windmill stood guard under a bold blue sky as he coaxed me into the water. I made a brave attempt to cut and lay the reeds, but had to borrow a few from Eric's healthy looking row to thump on a wooden board to level the cut ends of the stalks in the bundle.

'Comb out all the rubbish and tie 'em up if they are dry enough. You never tie them if they are wet; they'll only go mouldy.'

I worked overtime to keep up with instructions while Eric explained that alternate sides of the dyke were mown so some vegetation was always available for wildlife like the swallowtail butterfly and bearded tit. He pointed to a bank where trees were cut low. 'We're trying to get the bittern back here,' he said in a way that suggested it was only a matter of time.

He could see me struggling. 'I told you mowing was hard graft... come and have a rest in my shed,' smiled the natural communicator who enlightens hundreds of visiting schoolchildren every year, many of them sampling Norfolk's outdoor glories for the first time. His shed is an instant museum it has taken nearly thirty years to create.

We clambered over rat traps, coypu catchers and wire sparrow cages to reach a collection of tools used a century ago. The crome was employed to drag plants out of the dyke. A didle scooped up the mud. Inevitably he came back to the scythe, caressing it like an old friend. Nearby, leather reed-cutters' thigh boots glowed with pride. 'They were soled in 1911,' confided Eric.

He has been visited in his natural workplace by Prince Charles, Margaret Thatcher and Harry Secombe. He has appeared on television's *Generation Game* to demonstrate reed-cutting skills. He is a splendid ambassador for the Broads Authority at a time of great challenge and change:

> *I love chatting to people about the magic of this place. I see something new every day. Some say I work in a natural paradise and so I am insulated from changes going on in Norfolk and the rest of the world. But I see it simply as my job to carry on and do my little bit here.*
>
> *I want to leave something of interest and value for the next generations. Places like this will become even more important by the time we have raced into the next century. And I don't really mind if they keep laughing at me swinging a scythe. I'll just keep telling them the old ways are best.*

He swished contentedly as the water sucked at his boots and the old willows waved beyond the mill. I left him keeping a proud tradition alive in his little bit of paradise.

෴

16 *Belated Praise*

A sk anyone outside Norfolk for a list of important figures to emerge from the county over the centuries and many selections would include the likes of Boadicea, Edith Cavell, Elizabeth Fry, Robert Kett, Horatio Nelson, Thomas Paine, 'Turnip' Townshend and Robert Walpole.

Bringing the exercise more up to date could well prompt mentions of Cromer lifeboatman Henry Blogg, turkey tycoon Bernard Matthews, celebrity chef and Norwich City Football Club majority shareholder Delia Smith, actor and writer Stephen Fry and the good old Singing Postman, Allan Smethurst. They are still humming 'Hev You Gotta Loight, Boy?' way beyond Norfolk's passport control.

Of course, there have been many others causing waves or sending ripples past the county boundaries, but for one reason or another they have never been afforded the same sort of attention or credit. At the risk of prompting a few embarrassed glances across Norfolk's history pages, both from modest achievers and those who preferred to overlook them, I offer a few characters worthy of belated but sincere salutes.

Ebenezer Brewer (1810–1897) wrote a book which has sold several hundred thousand copies – and it is still in print. Beloved of authors, journalists, schoolteachers and anyone else fascinated by or curious about our wonderful language, it is *Brewer's Dictionary of Phrase and Fable*.

Ebenezer Cobham Brewer was the son of a Norwich schoolmaster and after a spell as a teacher he entered Trinity Hall, Cambridge in 1832. Four years later he was ordained a priest in Ely and became a Doctor of Law in 1840. A prolific writer who had published books while teaching in Norwich, he was a compulsive taker of notes 'on imaginary things' and so began his dictionary in 1860. No one was more surprised than he, except perhaps Cassell, his publisher, when it became an instant success. It sold 100 000 copies before it was revised in 1894, and has been a best-seller ever since.

Brewer's gift was to make available to a wide and predominantly self-educated working class public some of the more specialised results of a nineteenth century scholarship, and he wasn't afraid to be entertaining. A reference book which has flourished for well over a century is certainly something exceptional.

Mary Chapman (1647–1724) helped lay the foundations of modern mental health care with her progressive ideas. Mary was thirty-five when she became the second wife of the Revd Samuel Chapman, and one of the bonds that drew them together was the fact both had relatives who were mentally sick. When Samuel died he left in his will a sum of money to build 'a hospital for the habitation of poor lunatics, and not for natural-born fools or idiots'.

Mary accepted the task of building only the second mental health hospital in the country. The Bethel Hospital in Norwich opened in 1713 and was a most progressive institution for its time. For a start, the idea of mental unbalance being an illness was not generally acceptable. In most parts of the country lunatics were regarded as little better than criminals.

Patients in Norwich were offered facilities for recreation and worship, and the Bethel kept up with modern developments. The whole emphasis was on cure, and the hospital reported a rate of recovery in excess of 60 per cent at the start of the twentieth century. Today the Bethel Hospital is used to treat children and adolescents with psychiatric problems.

William D'Oyley (1745–1814) was highly unusual for his time – he cared about road safety. He remained a poor man all his life but luckily for Norwich and several villages around he put his own interests last. When he noticed a danger spot, like too steep a descent or a nasty bend, he mounted his horse and rode to all villages around to raise funds for improvements. He once collected enough money to have a hilly road near Tasburgh made more travel-friendly. In Norwich he noted the bottleneck in Brigg Street before it widened into the Haymarket and the Market Place. In all he rode an estimated 12 000 miles collecting money from surrounding villages to pay for improvements.

The poor parson rode the equivalent of 15 times the distance from Land's End to John o' Groats and didn't cut down the travelling in later life. Sadly, he didn't see many results for all his work as road improvements were a long time coming. But William D'Oyley pointed the way.

Sarah Glover (1786–1867) created the Tonic Sol-Fa system which achieved remarkable results with untrained singers. The best way to salute her work is to sing that song from *The Sound of Music*, the one that starts 'Doh, a deer, a female deer, Ray, a drop of golden sun...' Those sounds and the Me, Fah, Soh, Lah, Tee , Doh which follow form the Tonic Sol-Fa.

As she became interested in music this daughter of a Norwich clergyman considered the possibility of finding a single method of teaching both sight-reading and sight-singing. She started to teach from her own scale chart, which resembled a ladder and was later to be called a modulator. To modulate means to change from one key to another during the course of a piece of music, such a change being accomplished by a continuous musical means – that is not simply by starting afresh in another key.

Her pioneering work remained unknown outside local circles until 1841 when a young minister, the Revd John Curwen, was trying to find a simple way of teaching schools and congregations to sing music not only at sight but in time. He simplified and then commercialised Sarah's original idea. Sol-Fa classes sprang up all over the country and overseas as well. Between them they decided that the Norwich Sol-Fa system would become the Tonic Sol-Fa system, the names being still in existence today. Julie Andrews wasn't the only one to take advantage!

Luke Hansard (1752–1828) is the Norwich name behind official reports on proceeding of the House of Commons. Apprenticed to a printer on leaving school, young Hansard could soon manage typesetting, lay-out, press work and engraving. At eighteen he went to seek his fortune in London with just a guinea in his pocket.

A master printer at twenty-two, Luke climbed higher when his boss landed the contract for printing the *House of Commons Journal*, an unofficial account of proceedings written by radical William Cobbett. He published 6000 copies at one shilling (5p) each. Cobbett was a turbulent chap, often contemptuous of restrictive practices, and this brought him a three-year prison sentence in 1810.

By then Luke Hansard had become one of the big names in the business. The boy who arrived in the capital with a guinea died worth £80 000. His son, Thomas, bought Cobbett's *Journal* when the MP was in financial trouble during his spell in prison. The business remained in the hands of the family until 1889 when it was taken over by the Stationery Office. The name of Hansard was officially adopted for their reports in 1943.

George Manby (1765–1854) was a prolific inventor from West Norfolk who helped save thousands of lives – but never received the kind of rewards his efforts deserved. Born in Denver and educated at Downham Market, he died at Gorleston in his ninetieth year and is buried in Hilgay churchyard. He invented the rocket lifesaving apparatus as well as a chemical fire extinguisher, elastic sheets for use at fires, harpoons for whaling, improved types of lifeboats, howitzers and dredgers.

There is an impressive exhibition of his inventions in the Yarmouth Maritime Museum. A tablet on the back of his Gorleston home reads:

> *In commemoration of the 12th February, 1808, on which day directly eastwards of this site the first life was saved from shipwreck by means of a rope attached to a shot fired from a mortar over the stranded vessel, a method now universally adopted and to which at least 1,000 sailors of various nations owe their lives. 1848*

Manby complained often about the government's indifference to his inventions and thought Queen Victoria should have given him a knighthood. In 1803 he went to London to offer his services to the Secretary of War to assassinate Napoleon. He was refused – and instead was appointed Barracks Master at Great Yarmouth. It was here he witnessed a shipwreck involving the loss of 200 lives, a disaster that impelled him to develop his idea of a mortar-and-rocket apparatus for throwing a line from shore to ship. He came up with the first portable fire extinguisher in 1813 after seeing a blaze in an Edinburgh building where the firemen were unable to get their equipment to the upper floors.

Harriet Martineau (1802–1876) not only shone in the spheres of literature and politics, but scored personal triumphs over severe physical disabilities, poverty and misfortune. Born in Norwich, without the sensations of taste and smell, she was deaf by the time she was eighteen. Her father's business crashed in 1826 and the shock killed him. Harriet had been engaged but her fiancé died from a brain illness. Now acutely aware of the inadequacies and miseries of her fellows she began her lifelong study of social reform and political economy.

She went to America and her progressive mind found a new challenge in the slave question. She became a keen supporter of the Abolitionist party and the article published on her return to Britain in the *Westminster Review* introduced English readers to what she called 'The Martyr Age in the United States.' Struck down by a mystery complaint that confined her indoors for five years, she recovered sufficiently to become the first woman journalist to join a big London daily as leader writer for the *Daily News* in 1852.

A lucid thinker and fearless champion of any cause she pursued, Harriet suffered almost continuously from ill health – but never yielded to self-pity.

Kenneth McKee (1906–1990) pioneered one of modern medicine's most successful procedures, the artificial hip-joint operation. The Norwich surgeon first got the idea from car mechanics in the 1940s. He had to cope with much scepticism in his own profession before evidence of his work to bring relief from pain and new mobility to the formerly disabled proved too overwhelming to ignore.

He developed the idea on the principle of imitating the body's own ball and cup joint, designing replacement mechanisms and carrying out pioneering operations at the Norfolk and Norwich Hospital. The key to early success was cobalt-chrome, a metal which proved particularly suitable for use as an artificial joint. 'I used to take my motor bike to pieces and put it back together again, and do a lot on the car. And when you have a defective joint, as on a car, the obvious thing is to replace it,' was the straightforward McKee formula. He also developed replacement joints for knees and elbows and clamps for treating leg fractures.

When the revolutionary idea was first published in a paper and circulated among the medical profession, top surgeons from all over the world came to Norwich to learn about the technique. The idea was fully developed in the city in partnership with Dr John Farrar-Watson.

Nugent Monck (1878–1958) founded the Maddermarket Theatre in Norwich in 1921, and helped it build up an international reputation. A former Roman Catholic chapel, which had been used as a warehouse and Salvation Army Citadel at the turn of the twentieth century, it was transformed into a delightful Elizabethan theatre for £3300.

The productions, settings and costumes were of a high standard, and Monck's reign lasted until his retirement in 1952. He produced all of Shakespeare's plays between 1921 and 1932, and he wasn't above cutting out whole scenes and inventing linking passages of his own. The son of a Shropshire clergyman, Monck was a martinet on stage, accustomed to giving orders and having them obeyed. He once said, 'Anyone who wants to act for me must bring unquestioning obedience and his own greasepaint...' He turned down countless invitations for his Norwich Players to tour abroad – 'if people want to see us badly enough they can make the pilgrimage' – but he did lecture for the British Council in Germany and the West Indies. He was made an OBE in 1946 and was given a CBE shortly before his death.

Fuller Pilch (1804–1870) was the top batsman in England for well over a decade. Born in the small village of Horningtoft, near Fakenham, he was lured away from the Norfolk cricket scene to Kent in 1836 by an offer of £100 a year. He played on until he was fifty-one, helping to restore Kent's status as a force in the game. The Earl of Besborough, who played alongside him, said, 'I always put Pilch and Grace in a class by themselves, and I put them very much on a level.'

While with Norfolk, for whom his brothers Nathaniel and William also played, Pilch scored emphatic victories over Yorkshireman Tom Marsden, the national single-wicket champion. Pilch won by an innings and 70 runs in Norwich and by 127 runs in Sheffield. In 1834, before Pilch went to Kent, Norfolk beat Yorkshire in what was probably the first county match to be played in Norwich. Pilch made 87 not out, and 73.

In retirement, Fuller Pilch kept the Saracen's Head pub in Canterbury, and is reputed to have refused all appeals for credit as he did for leg before wicket when umpiring, scornfully crying, 'Bowl 'em out!'

Derek and Hugh Seagrim, their exploits marked on the village sign in their home patch of Whissonsett, are the only brothers to win the country's top two awards for bravery.

Lt-Col Derek Seagrim took command of the 7th Battalion Green Howards for the Western Desert campaign in the Second World War. During the offensive at the Mareth Line he accounted for 20 of the enemy, totally disregarding his own safety and setting an outstanding example to his own men. However, he died of his wounds and in May, 1943 the posthumous award of the Victoria Cross was announced. His mother, Mrs Amelia Seagrim went to Buckingham Palace to receive the decoration from the king.

Three years later, Mrs Seagrim made history when she again went to the Palace to receive a posthumous award. This time it was the George Cross awarded to Major Hugh Seagrim in recognition of his work and self-sacrifice in Burma. He loved the Karen people and it was to save them brutal persecution from the Japanese that he surrendered in 1944. After enduring long periods of solitary confinement he was executed by the Japanese.

Doreen Wallace (1897–1989) gained national recognition in a forty-year battle to abolish what she described as 'the iniquitous tithe tax'. She wrote over 50 books under the pen-name of Doreen Wallace – her real name was Doreen Rash.

A former landowner and farmer at Wortham, near Diss, she became President of the National Tithe Payers' Association, and in 1934 she and her husband barricaded their farm during a six-week siege after her refusal to pay the Church of England tithe. Eventually 134 pigs and 15 cattle worth £700 were seized in lieu of the tax, and a memorial recording that event was erected. In the summer of 1939 she decided to see if the Church really would make a person bankrupt – so she refused to pay again.

This time her furniture and bedding were taken from her home and auctioned. But the auctioneer was a close friend and the furniture was bought by other members of the Association. The payment, traditionally one tenth of a landowner's profits, had to be paid to the Church and was later collected by the Inland Revenue. It was abolished in 1967.

On her death at ninety-two, the *Eastern Daily Press* called her:

> ... *a latter-day Boadicea – here was no ordinary lady of the manor. Doreen Wallace remained a trenchant East Anglian non-conformist of the secular kind almost up to the end of her life.*

∞

17 Deep Pockets

I went looking for pockets of resistance – and found them deep and well-lined with experience, knowledge and unfading humour. Hundreds of Norfolk words and expressions still doing the regular rounds came my way at the start of the twenty-first century when I launched a campaign to test dialect waters.

It wasn't so much an in-depth survey as an amiable reunion of those who felt our vernacular retained a colourful and valuable place on an increasingly sophisticated communications agenda. Many contributors admitted they were 'bilingual', employing both orthodox English and Broad Norfolk when occasions demanded. This sort of versatility was evident well over a century ago, especially in rural areas, so there's no need today to feel guilty or exceptional.

Thomas Hardy captured the state of affairs well in *Tess of the d'Urbevilles* in 1891 when he wrote:

> *Mrs Durbeyfield habitually spoke the dialect; her daughter, who had passed the Sixth Standard in the National School under a London-trained mistress, spoke two languages – the dialect at home, more or less ordinary English abroad and to persons of quality.*

Yes, the Norfolk dialect will continue to be diluted. It will have to adapt to even more challenge and change. A host of delightful words and expressions spoken by Norfolk parents and grandparents disappeared with trades and pursuits that inspired them. While horses ruled the furrows for much of the first part of the twentieth century, the horsemen and those who worked in associated jobs like the blacksmith had a language of their own. 'Go an' fetch the dutfin for the ole hoss,' would lead to a bridle or halter. I was a 'hold-ye boy' in charge of the horses drawing loads of corn sheaves in the harvest field and warning the man on top of the load to hold tight. Some called it a 'howd-gee boy', but it amounted to the same thing.

We echo a few of these gems out of sheer sentiment and to underline a sad sense of loss. Then we wonder if a world of computers, mobile phones and plastic cards can leave a local linguistic legacy of any kind. It seems highly doubtful as we are urged to think global.

In the meantime, Norfolk dialect enthusiasts can celebrate the strength of and affection for something supposed to have been on its last legs decades ago, although it is wise to be wary of staking sole claims on certain items. Several favourites enjoy a wider currency. For example, we sigh 'Thass gittin' wholly dark over Will's Mother's' as bad weather approaches, but this old lady's influence is not confined to Norfolk. Similarly, it is not only Norfolk children who are told they can go out to play if there's enough blue sky to make a sailor a pair of trousers. And venerable citizens well beyond the county boundaries have been heard to mutter 'Rain before seven, fine before eleven.'

Wit and wisdom laced many contributions with a potent Norfolk flavour, some clearly exclusive to one particular locality or family. The art of homely corruption continues to put new smiles on well-known proverbs. "He who laughs last didn't get the joke in the first place' and 'Never do today what you can put off until tomorrow' are good examples from that department. Dialect fun and games come to the fore in gems like 'Be sparin' when there's a'plenty, an' yew'll still hev sum when there ent nun!' and 'Never yew mind where I live ... dew yew cum a' see me!'

There were several references to someone being called a 'half-sixer', a derogatory term usually applied to a rather pretentious person. It may have come from 'half-past six', suggesting the individual would remain in bed for half an hour after the working man began his labours.

'He think he is but he ent, y'know!' and 'She wuz put in wi' the bread an' taken out wi' the cakes' are other useful put-downs to those putting on airs.

The subtle art of dishing out insults without giving too much offence can reach a peak when couched in Norfolk humour and dialect. 'He dunt git no farther than Wednesday' and 'If his hid wuz a gun that wunt blow his cap orff' are popular examples of describing someone a bit on the educationally challenged side. They make the point without being too cruel. A few others from a big selection:

- She's got a fearce like a paralysed pork cheese.
- She kin tork the hind leg orff a dickey.
- If she breathed on yar chips, yew wunt need vinegar.
- He run on like a five bob watch.
- He's as much use as a yard o' pump water.
- If the wind changed, his fearce wunt take any notice.
- He look as thow he got up afore he went anywhere.
- He git vartigo on bottom rung o'the ladder.
- She dunt know which way her backside hang.
- He's about as sharp as a pound o'wet leather.
- He's got a Player accent an' a Woodbine packet.
- I wunt believe him if he said 'goodnyte'.
- He're got short arms an' deep pockets.

Older natives recall childhood days with grandparents when they heard expressions long since gone out of fashion. One said her gran would be most concerned if the vicar, or anyone else of note, called in the morning when she was 'in my dissables'. Well, that comes from the French 'deshabille' which means being only partly or carelessly dressed, hardly the best state in which to greet parson or squire! Many a mawther embarrassed at being caught in such disarray on washing day made sure she was smartly attired after lunch.

How did such a fashionable French word find its way to Norfolk in the first place? Perhaps it came with the influx of Dutch and Walloon weavers. By the start of the seventeenth century it is estimated one third of the population of Norwich was of foreign origins. The majority of the 'Strangers' spoke Dutch, but there were French-speaking Walloons among them, and there was also a smaller number of Huguenots driven out of France in the seventeenth century. The word 'lucom', an attic window, or one of those hooded projections from old mills and warehouses where sacks of grain were hoisted by a pulley and chain to the top floor, clearly comes from the French *lucarne*. 'Plancher', old Norfolk for floor, is also of French origin, and there's another intriguing connection when it comes to eighteenth century sanitary arrangements in Norwich.

Housewives used to empty slops out of the upper windows of the old overhanging houses into the drains running down the centre of the narrow cobbled streets. They shouted 'gardiloo!' (*garde à vous*) to warn folk in the street below.

Even those who find our dialect difficult to grasp can appreciate the traditional way of finding out if a person comes from Norfolk. A question posed as a test during the First World War is still being employed.

A Norfolk nurse, thinking she recognised a wounded soldier as coming from her home village, whispered in his ear: 'Ha' yer fa'r got a dickey, bor?'. He knew that meant 'Has your father got a donkey, boy?' and mumbled through his bandages, 'Yis, an' he want a fule ter roide 'im, will yew cum?.' That means, 'Yes, and he wants a fool to ride him, will you come?.' On bumping into each other far from home, Norfolk people still use that question and answer as recognition signals.

I was genuinely heartened by such widespread interest in the dialect and all its derivations and uses, an interest helping to build big hopes for the future as well as pointing to affection for the past. The formation of FOND, Friends Of Norfolk Dialect, in 1999 put that concern on an official footing for the first time, and a flourishing organisation is working hard to promote and preserve this vital strand of our cultural heritage. Many Norfolk exiles play important roles with 'missionary work' in other parts of the country.

My personal campaign to test those dialect waters could only act as a rough guide, but even hardened cynics must accept that it is too strong, too precious to let go. Here are lists of favourite Norfolk words and expressions to emerge from my six-month exercise sifting through thousands of contributions:

FAVOURITE WORDS
Allust (always), **blar** (cry), **bishy-barney-bee** (ladybird), **buskins** (leather leggings), **corf** (cough), **cuckoo** (cocoa), **datty** (dirty), **dickey** (donkey), **dodman** (snail), **dwile** (floor cloth), **dudder** (shiver), **fang** (seize), **fewl** (fool), **gansey** (jersey), **garp** (stare), **harnser** (heron), **jiffle** (fidget), **mardle** (to gossip), **mawkin** (scarecrow), **mawther** (girl), **muckwash** (hot and bothered), **puckaterry** (muddle), **shud** (shed), **slarver** (talk rubbish), **smur** (light rain), **squit** (nonsense), **swidge** (small puddle), **tricolate** (repair or decorate), **troshin'** (threshing), **wholly** (very).

TOP EXPRESSIONS
• Thass a lot o' ole squit!
• Don't yew be ser bloomin' sorft!
• I'm fair ter middlin' thankyer.

- Hold yew hard, my ole bewty!
- He're got suffin' gorn abowt.
- That'll be a nice day if that dunt rain.
- Cor blarst … I'll square yew up!
- Stop puttin' yar parts on.
- Are yew now a'cummin'?
- I'll dew it now, directly.
- That took me best part o'sum tyme.
- Thass a rum ole dew!
- Dew yew lissun here!
- Wuh, thass on the huh.
- That'll larn yer!
- She never med a deen.
- Dunt yew hull that away.
- Fare y'well, tergether!

෨෪

18 *Tall Stories*

I have enjoyed tall stories ever since an old Norfolk boy on the farm told me he had discovered a cow's nest.

Following him in keen anticipation of extending my grasp of nature study beyond the bike shed academy, I had the good sense to laugh as he unravelled six empty milk bottles in the hedge.

That was by no means the last time I fell for a spot of rustic leg-pulling, but it did put me on my guard when the harvest crew asked for volunteers to fetch a pail of dry water. And I knew that making the wire-netting slope was no guarantee of keeping rain off the chickens.

Squit among the haystacks. Useful preparation for a scrawny lad with literary ambitions. 'Sharpen yar wits as well as yar pencils!' called that old boy with a proclivity for finding things in hedges as I walked away one late summer's morning. It all came back across the stubble of time as I sat reading an old magazine specialising in country matters.

The tall story to catch my eye concerned a man who could get you just about anything. They used to call them higglers or 'little do-ers' in Norfolk, although it was not unknown for magistrates to pin other labels on them in certain cases.

One day, two smart-looking gents approached our rural all-rounder in the pub and said they wanted a hare for coursing. He promised to get them one within hours. He caught one, killed it, skinned it and then sewed the skin on a cat. He put the cat in a cage and sent a message to the men that he had managed to obtain them a hare.

'Bring your dogs,' he said. They did, and the party went to the bottom of a field, this chap with the 'hare' in a sack. When he let it go, they let their dogs go. The pursued animal went straight up a tree.

'These gentlemen had never seen a hare go up a tree before, and for all I know they're still trying to make their friends believe it!'"

John Gray, of Pulham Market, provided a running commentary for his entry in the Tall Story Stakes:

'My old grandfather was a bit of a jockey and he used to go in for all the local steeplechases. He had some rum horses but the best was a mare called Old Sal. Fair fly, she could.

'He entered her for a race at Yarmouth and then found she was heavily in foal. Howsomever, he saddled her up and lined up with the rest. Because of her condition he got good long odds.

'The starter dropped his flag and off they went. By the third fence Old Sal was well ahead, but after the fourth she suddenly stopped. Grandfather jumped off her back. Old Sal lay down on the ground, gave a groan – and out popped a lovely little foal.

'Old Sal got up and gave the foal a quick lick. Grandfather jumped back in the saddle and off they went. By this time the rest of the field were well ahead but by the last fence Old Sal was up with the leaders.

'Do you know, she won that race by a short head…

'And that little foal, he came in third!'

⌒

Two lads from Bungay missed the last bus home after a Saturday night out in Norwich.

'We'll hatter go up the bus station an' tearke one hoom ourselves,' suggested Billy. So his mate Horry climbed up the wall in Surrey Street and dropped down the other side. He was gone for the best part of some time.

'What are you a'dewin'?' shouted Billy.

'I'm a'lookin' for a bus what say thass goin' ter Bungay,' replied Horry.

'Don't you be ser sorft,' shouted Billy. 'What do that matter?' He vaulted over the wall and soon spotted a bus showing Woodton on its destination board, a village a few miles from Bungay.

'There we are, bor,' he said with relief. 'We'll tearke this one. But we'll hatter get out at Woodton an' walk the rest o' the way.'

⌒

Jacob had to move from his beloved Norfolk countryside in his later years to live with his daughter in London. He couldn't acclimatise to life in the big city. He fell ill and it soon became clear he had reached his final innings.

The family gathered round the bed. 'What can we do for you?' they asked.

'Only thing what'll dew me any good now is a drop o'Norfolk air,' murmured the old man.

'Don't you fret,' said son-in-law Fred. 'I'll see to that.'

Next day, Fred got his bike out and set off for Norfolk. He reached Norwich Cattle Market on the Saturday morning. There he let the wind out of his tyres, pumped them up again and headed back to London.

Opening his front door he took the bike inside and carried it up the stairs. 'Here comes the boy Fred,' they cried. 'You'll soon be all right, now, Jacob.'

Fred bent down, unscrewed the valve and let all the wind out of the tyre. Old Jacob propped himself up on a pillow, took one whiff – and passed away.

'Oh, dear,' exclaimed his daughter. 'I don't understand that. I thought it would do him some good.'

'Yes,' said Fred. 'It's a great pity I got that puncture in Colchester.'

෴

A holidaymaker and a local had been fishing on opposite banks of the river at Horning on the Norfolk Broads. They met in the local pub that evening.

The holidaymaker greeted the local angler and said, 'I caught a roach today and it was three feet long. How did you get on?'

The old Norfolk boy drained his glass, pushed it across the counter, smiled and scratched his head. 'Dew yew know I pulled out an old lantern. 'Bowt a thousand years old, that wuz. I'll tell you suffin else. That wuz still alight.'

The visitor was taken aback, not least because it was the done thing for the angler who had fared best to buy the next round. 'What are we going to do about it?' he asked.

'Well, ole partner,' replied the Norfolk sage. 'It you take two foot off yar roach, I'll blow the light out in my lantern!'

෴

Bertie was very fond of his pet canary. He let it out of the cage every day to spread its wings in a flight round the kitchen. One day it was frightened by the cat and flew up the chimney. When it came down it was heavily coated in soot.

Bertie decided to wash the canary with the aid of a much-advertised soap powder. In walked Bertie's brother Fred, who was not at all convinced the soap powder would do the trick. In fact, he prophesied the bird would die.

Next day Bertie told Fred the canary was dead. With much sarcasm Fred said he knew that would be the result. Bertie put him right.

'Blarst no, bor. That wunt the soap powder what dunnit … that wuz the mangle!'

⟲

The farmer and his wife carried a milk churn into the bank at Fakenham and took it up to the counter.

'What with all them burglaries about we thowt we'd better start a bank account,' said the farmer, removing the lid to show the churn was full of coins. It took the cashier some time to count it all out. When she said how much there was the farmer looked alarmed.

'That can't be right,' he said. 'Thass abowt fifteen pound short.'

Suddenly, his wife went red. 'Yew know what we hev done, dunt yew?' she said. 'We hev gorn an' brought the wrong churn!'

⟲

A Norfolk farmer sent his foreman to borrow a cross-cut saw … his mangolds were so big he couldn't get them into the cart. Off went the foreman.

'Please, sar, my marster would like ter borrer yar crors-cut saw. His mangles are so big he can't lift 'em inter the cart.'

'Well, bor,' replied the neighbour, 'Dew yew tell yar marster I'm wholly sorry but my crors-cut happen ter be stuck in one o'my taters.'

⟲

Jack was strolling across the field when he saw Stan hoeing the sugar beet.

'What time dew yew knock orff?'

'Five o'clock.'

'Hev yew got a watch?'

'No, I hent got a watch.'

'So how dew yew know when thass time ter pack up?'

'Well, yew see that railway line over there … a train go past at half past five, so if I pack up half an hour afore that git here, I know I'm right.'

This come comes from the 'it really did happen' file. It features a man who married for the second time the day before his first wife was buried…

The episode was recalled by Edward 'Dick' Kendal of Dereham nearly fifty years ago and appeared in the *Dereham and Fakenham Times*. He was then verger at St Nicholas parish church at Dereham, but his family came from Guist.

It was in this village at the end of the nineteenth century that his great-uncle Daniel Kendal married his second wife and then buried his first. It happened like this.

As a young man Daniel was a bank clerk at Holt. He got bored with the job. Accompanied by another man and their respective wives he emigrated and took up ranching on the Argentine plains.

Sadly, the climate did not agree with the women and both died two years later. There was no church anywhere near Mr Kendal's isolated shack so he constructed a box and buried his wife near the walls.

His friend became homesick and returned to England, but Daniel remained there for twenty years until he had made enough money to retire and return to Guist. He would not leave his wife's remains in unconsecrated ground. So he dug up the box, encased it in another one and packed it off to his brother and sister-in-law at Guist.

Dick Kendal's grandmother kept the box under her bed out of the way of inquisitive sons until the emigrant returned home. Daniel married a childhood friend from Swanton Novers – and then the remains of the first Mrs Kendal were interred in the churchyard at Guist.

∞

19 *Futility Rites*

For reasons that could be tied up with the binder twine holding up my trousers, or the length of straw permanently jutting out of the corner of my mouth, I am taken often as an expert on quaint old Norfolk customs.

I tell those who ask that we still hold the odd Coronation street party, Jubilee tea and Thanksgiving supper to mark the end of a war or the start of a new blackberry-picking season. We also celebrate openly when a whooping cough epidemic is wiped out. It all stems from an age when we had to make our own amusements to complement the regular rhythms of a Norfolk largely at ease with itself. Communities were small and closely-knit, bound to the soil and the eternal secrets of overgrown headlands and bountiful hedgerows.

Ironically, country life has lost much of its spontaneity while demands for it to be revived are on the increase. New villagers, invariably drawn by ancient tales of rustic rituals designed to keep indigenous folk out of mischief before satellite dishes, mobile phones, real ale, paintball in the forest and growing genetically-modified cucumbers, hunger for the old anniversaries and antics.

Now that the corn harvest, the coronation of the year, can just about be wrapped up in the space of a journey to and from the supermarket, there's a natural urge to send for the scythe and sickle to reap a few golden memories lingering beyond the stubble. I point to the old Norfolk custom of Ten Pounding as a shining example of how we used to look after each other as the sun dipped and the stack rose.

Any worker caught contravening the harvest rules was subjected to a swift court-martial. If found guilty he was seized and thrown down flat on his back. A report from some bucolic Harry Carpenter at the rural ringside continues:

Some of the party keep his head down and confine his arms, while others turn up his legs in the air so as to exhibit his posterior. The person who is to inflict the punishment then takes a shoe, and with the heel of it (studded as it usually is with hob nails) gives him the prescribed number of blows upon his breech, according to the sentence.

The rest of the party sit by, with their hats off, to see that the executioner does his duty; and if he fails in this, he undergoes the same punishment. It sometimes happens that, from the prevailing use of high-lows (ankle boots) a shoe is not be found among the company. In this case the hardest and heaviest hand of the reap is selected for the instrument of correction, and when it is laid on with a hearty good will it is not inferior to the shoe.

Instant healthy justice, methinks, largely confined these days to the odd Cabinet reshuffle or sacking of a football manager about to experience the opposite of being 'over the moon'. Shame on those who suggest it could be one of the reasons behind dwindling numbers of workers on the land. A good shoe across the backside never did me any harm!

My good friend, modest folk-singing megastar Sid Kipper, is a real expert on our old customs, and he does a splendid job as Norfolk's main cultural ambassador in the guise of a leading member of the East Anglian Anti-Tourist Board.

Sid first brought to national attention our penchant for Junepole dancing, clearest indication yet that Norfolk has no qualms about being slightly behind the times. And Sid knows just how busy the merry month of May can be with all its rituals and incantations. His May to Z is a veritable storehouse of staggeringly simple explanations for certain words and expressions – that is, once they have been stripped of their traditional mystique and modern misrepresentation.

For example, May Hem, according to sagacious Sid, is the hem of the May Queen's skirt, and the first three young men to touch it become May Kings. These three Kings are known as the May Ji.

Now everyone wants to be a May King. So as the May Queen appears at dawn all the young men rush and fight and push to touch the hem of her skirt – that's what they call Mayhem. Of course, after that there's no special reason for touching the May Queen's hem. Any girl's hem will do, and they grab hold and won't let go. That's known as Hemlock.

The Kipper kaleidoscope embraces many other splendid elucidations as he sizes up the month described by Chaucer's maternal grandfather as 'thatte Maylstrum of Nayture's juwses'. May Cup, May Dew, May Kit, May Tree Arc, May Tricks, the highly secretive May Suns and May Zing all blossom with fresh meaning. There's even a place for May-on-Naze, 'a small village halfway between Ross-on-Wye and Eccles-on-Sea'.

Now and again, Norfolk has to put out a welcome mat fashioned from grudging acceptance that not everyone will believe rumours about the countryside being noisy, brutal and full. I recall a visit from a sort of modern Clement Scott working for one of those posh Sunday newspapers determined to send all its readers to the same spot to find rural tranquillity. Here's a sample of his poetic offering:

> *Hayblown lanes by day and salt-scented waterways at night help us to reassess our sympathies and antipathies and to relearn the grammar of a mystic communion we are forced to shun in the shouting capital.*

Exactly. Nothing we like better than a good old mystic reunion, even if we're not always prepared for prying eyes, flapping ears and wagging tongues as we commune mystically on our own midden at Cold Comfort Farm. Sitting cross-legged on the edge of a sugar beet field, calling upon the rustic god Horry Krishna to protect the crop, can do more damage to your loincloth and buskins than to your image if the weather should turn contrary.

Shaking a bottle of cold tea to check how quickly the dregs can resettle, and then chanting an ancient agricultural prayer over a razor-sharp beet hook, may not be everyone's idea of fun on a raw November morning.

Still, there are certain rituals we like to sustain, if only to prove to ourselves that the dark, dreary days towards the tail end of the year can be just as uplifting, equally as important in the great order of things as those sap-rising, sukebind-budding, soul-enhancing spring mornings when it is so easy to yield to Mother Nature's pull.

Fine weather is a must for dwile flonking, easily the most noble and character-building of our local rites. Its origins are lost in the mists of time – some enthusiasts claim it goes back to the early 1950s – but regular revivals point to its potency as a pastime for those who love a mixture of ale and action, beer and bonhomie.

A couple of years ago it became clear to me how far this rousing recreation can go when I helped forge a link between Norfolk and the

Land of the Rising Sun. A writer in London was approached by some Japanese connections for details of quaint old English customs. Naturally, he phoned the Tourist Information Office in Cromer to ask if they could unravel the splendours of dwile flonking.

They called me and I passed on all I knew. Hopes remain high that it will find favour in Japan. Here's a summary of the rules as compiled by the Waveney Valley Dwile Flonking Association:

Each team consists of eight players in yokel attire. They form a circle around one of the opposing team. When the referee gives the traditional shout of 'Here you go, tergether!' the player in the circle takes a dwile (floorcloth or dishcloth) from the bucket of ale and places it on the end of his driveller, a pole used to project the dwile. This act is called flonking.

The encircled player shouts 'Dwiles Away!' and spins round. With a flick of his driveller he projects the dwile towards the circle.

He flonks two dwiles. If he scores with both efforts he receives a bonus dwile. While the flonker in the middle is spinning, the circle can move round, up and down, but may not break the circle.

Scoring is as follows:
WONTON – this applies when the dwile strikes one of the encircling team on the head. Three points.
MORTHER – when the dwile strikes a player on the chest. Two points.
RIPPER – a hit below the belt. One point.
SWADGER – this term applies when the dwile hits none of the opponents in the circle. The referee shouts 'Swadger!' and the circle moves back and forms a straight line.

The flonker is handed a chamber pot of ale. As soon as he starts drinking the dwile is passed along the line of opponents who utter the ceremonial chant of 'Pot, pot, pot'. If the flonker fails to consume all the ale by the time the dwile has been passed along the entire line, his/her team loses three points.

The entire procedure is then repeated by the other team, and the side with most points wins the contest. An extra point is added to a team's score for every player still sober.

The referee's decision is final. He has the right to send any player off the field.

I've had the pleasure of refereeing one of these contests, and found that abstinence and a sou'wester keeps the brain sharp enough to implement complex rules firmly but fairly.

20 *Culinary Treat*

Norfolk's stock in the culinary world has risen dramatically since Delia Smith became a majority shareholder at Carrow Road in a bid to find a winning recipe for the Canaries.

Her involvement with Norwich City Football Club inevitably attracted many other celebrity chefs to this part of the world – although the natives were quick to point out that wholesome, old-fashioned food has always rated high on the social menu.

Nothing was wasted by country householders, and it was traditional to simmer a pig's head or extremities until very tender and then set the meat in its own jelly. The dish, known as brawn, dates from medieval times when it was served soused in a sharp vinegar sauce. In Norfolk the dish is known as pork cheese.

The people of Norfolk are often known as 'dumplings' in honour of their favourite food as well as their solidarity and firmness. The true Norfolk dumpling is made with a bread dough containing yeast or with a simple mixture of flour and water. It is known as a floater. Dumplings made of suet are known as sinkers or swimmers.

Samphire, generally referred to as poor man's asparagus, is a marsh plant that looks like seaweed and grows on the edge of tidal waters and marshes. Traditionally it was pickled to last through the winter after being gathered during July and August.

Best cockles in Norfolk are said to come from Stiffkey and are known as Stewkey Blues because of their grey-blue shells. The herring made Yarmouth famous. Cromer is noted for crabs. Young swans used to be a local delicacy and could still be obtained up until the 1930s.

With some of these tasty ingredients in mind, I set about putting together my favourite Norfolk meal – taking one or two liberties with village place names and items of blessed memory. Something here to suit all tastes … a bit like dear old Norfolk itself.

SKIPPER'S DELIGHT

Starter – Coypu Soup with little bits of bread floating on top
(only when Coypu is in season)
Alternatives – Egmere-onaise or Wighton-bait

Fish Course – Yarmouth Kippers
(specially prepared by Scottish fishergirls)

Main Course – Roasted Great Bustard with Sprouts, Turnips and
Parsnips
(only when Great Bustard is available in quantity)
Alternative – Cromer Shelduck in a nest of fresh samphire, crabsticks
and Paston lettuce.
(Local advice for cooking shelduck: 'Dew yew put a brick in th'oven
along wi' the bird. When the brick is sorft … so is the shelduck!')
Another Alternative – Jugged ferret
All the above can be served with Norfolk Dumplings, preferably
sinkers, or Stewkey Blues.

Dessert – Fair Buttons, flavoured with ginger and served with stewed
bullaces
Norfolk Biffin windfalls from Syderstone

Beverages – Home brewed Sugar Beet Wine, Trunch Punch, Barney
Beer, Castle Riesling or a cup o' cuckoo

Selection of local cheeses including Wendlingdale, Cheddargrave and
Mousehold.

Coffee and After Nine mints (Norfolk people often stay up late)

If you are still peckish, the sweet trolley can bring you a choice of
Eccles Cakes, Hethersett Jellies, Marsham-mallows or Pudding
Norton.

Toast – burnt

Entertainment – a big helping of Norfolk squit.

21 *Diehard Spirit*

I reckon it's inevitable that as Norfolk continues to change character so quickly; old-fashioned natives should be even more defiant in calls to leave well alone.

The diehard spirit must be strongest among those who can make comparisons. I wish I'd counted the number of times this sigh-laden comment has come my way over the years, 'I wander down the street and I don't recognise half the people I meet.' Not just fondness for closer-knit times but also a sad little commentary on a basic lack of communication in a busier and brasher world.

There are faults on both sides of the fence. The native bemoans the apparent coldness of the newcomer without seeing fit to inspire any warmth. The newcomer complains about difficulties in getting through that notorious Norfolk reserve without attempting to understand the reasons behind it.

Many true locals do display an automatic aversion to change and are at their most belligerent when alterations look like being imposed on them. Communities have been drained of the self-sufficiency and constancy that ran through them before the last war, but the yearning for what they meant still carries powerful pull.

Perhaps the concept is valid but the context now cruelly out of focus. Dismiss it as rank nostalgia if you like and then consider some of the 'magnets' drawing so many settlers and holidaymakers to this neck of the woods. If the Norfolk diehard is preoccupied with sepia-tinted pictures of the past, his new companions are ready fodder for the glossy brochures and slick estate-agent jargon of the present. Who is to say one is more impressionable than the other?

Norfolk is part of a region full of Eastern promise for those who want to get out of the London rat-race or the depression of places where manufacturing industries have been ground down. Despite recent leaps, property is still relatively cheap. Much of the immigration is retirement-led but there are many new ventures and new jobs flying in the face of traditional images that could well have lured people here in the first place. That's an irony refusing to be lost on the more sensitive native.

Tolerance tests must multiply as the old thatcher bumps into the computer analyst at a village social and the retired roadman shares a pew with the city commuter at the parish church.

I was chewing this theme over at a harvest supper when any inspection of credentials would have revealed only a handful of patrons who had even set foot in a cornfield since the combines started rolling. Of course, we can't reduce it all to the level of the ration book – so many coupons to gain you entry to certain events – simply because there are so few people left concerned with what some of us still regard as 'backbone' activities.

Even so, I think the Norfolk countryman ought to command respect for his unfading delight in harvests when the whole community took part. For him those memories are vivid and real. For so many others they are second-hand images out of a scrapbook.

Harvest togetherness was as tight as any binder twine round a shock of corn. That sort of togetherness is fast disappearing over the headlands and any function to recall it and to praise it can bring as much hurt as happiness.

The comparison factor is crucial to this debate. For instance, most newcomers say Norfolk roads are quaint and quiet and in dire need of improvement. The native will emphasise how much quainter and quieter they used to be and turn unhesitatingly to the latest accident figures as one of the inevitable prices to pay for progress so far.

Fingers may be pointed at a farming scene revolutionised by technology, taking the drudgery out of all the seasons and increasing efficiency. The old farm worker will query the value of over-production, glare at the countless spots where hedges have been ripped up and sympathise with his modern counterpart as he plies a lonely trade across the prairie.

As demand grows for holiday homes and weekend retreats the property market could 'catch up' with other areas – a doubtful distinction for young couples hoping to set up house not far from where parents and grandparents made their nests.

Tourism moguls seek out untapped parts for exploitation, careful to highlight the number of jobs the exciting project might bring. A precious environment, like parts of Breckland, becomes a battlefield. Bound to be ugly scars before many more rounds are over.

It's an over-simplification to bill this whole business as a sort of civil war between the Old Roundheads from the backwoods and the New Cavaliers from outside. I know many comparative newcomers to Norfolk are just as concerned about the county's future as the diehard battalion who started digging in as soon as the Vikings dropped in for a mardle.

However, the Norfolk character survival programme will ultimately flourish or fall on the efforts of those who can make comparisons.

If they can till enough common ground between yesterday's meadows and tomorrow's dual carriageways there's just a chance we'll recognise the old place when we're all drawing pensions.

∾

22 The Way Ahead

One thing is certain. Norfolk will continue to be a priority target for all kinds of solace-seekers despite its blatant shortcomings.

Dreadful roads. Insomniac cockerels. Sluggish tractors. Steaming manure. Awkward natives. Crumbling cliffs. Septic tanks. Dodgy signposts. A wonder anyone wants to take the risk of jumping out of the urban frying-pan into the rural fire, either for a weekend singe or a rest-of-lifetime roasting. But joyfully jump they will in their thousands, flattening a few hundred more hedgehogs, rabbits and pheasants daring to venture out onto a quiet lane leading to the rose-covered cottage where dreams come true.

A few with long-term aspirations will own up after one sultry summer or wicked winter and turn their backs on pastoral pleasures. Most will stick it out come hell or high water – speciality of the house at Happisburgh and a few other coastal locations – and encourage their city relatives and friends to take the plunge and join the happy trek. Norfolk isn't sold by smart estate agents organising roadshows in London, Leicester and Long Melford. It's Auntie Mabel and Cousin Claude singing 'All Things Bright and Beautiful' down the phone from Dunsweatin' and Dinglenook that keeps the inward traffic flowing.

On the basis that the Norfolk Independence Party (Nips) could find it difficult to defy the European Court of Human Rights when it comes to restriction on numbers and protection of areas of outstanding natural booty, it seems pertinent to suggest a mutually acceptable code of conduct as growth goes on. Native, newcomer and fleeting tripper must find some common ground and fertilise it regularly with straightforward but effective regulations.

Native demands come first simply because they are more important than anything else likely to surface in this campaign for peaceful co-existence, and there has to be some kind of reward for staying put and radiating satisfaction with the same place for a long while. It is rapidly becoming a forsaken art and a few forward-thinking folk (bred and born in the county and therefore ideal for the task) are preparing a consultation paper which proposes double payment of council tax for second-homers and handsome concessions for faithful residents who have lived in the same house or immediate area for twenty years or more. A clear incentive to foster extra community spirit.

Another idea already drawing solid support is that all those seeking the honour of representing Norfolk at Westminster should reside for a minimum of five years in the constituency they want to send them there. This is a logical move to prevent a well-educated, well-spoken, well-meaning candidate plucked from the Surrey stockbroker belt spending valuable time trying to find out what a honeycart is, what crab boats do and why the nit-nurse should return to her round of Norfolk schools.

This exciting brand of reasonably radical thinking should help break down barriers and build useful bridges to clearer understanding. There's no better way of currying favour with Norfolk people than to accept they are different from the start and praise them openly for it instead of criticising behind their backs.

Another good tip to forestall open hostilities – newcomers and visitors ought to deliberately mis-pronounce Norfolk words and place names, especially in Happisburgh, Hautbois and Hargham, to give the local a clear psychological advantage. Tired old jokes about passports, drawbridges, turkeys, ferrets down trousers, crawling tractors and close-knit families should be kept firmly under wraps until a clear rapport has been developed.

Pub conversations should avoid references to housing estates, hypermarkets, more dual carriageways, street lights, Estuary English, electrified commuters and Ipswich Town FC. All wishing to settle in the county or pay regular calls must agree Norfolk people possess a marvellous sense of humour, even if all evidence occasionally points to the contrary. It is best to ride with the drollery, the glorious understatement of Norfolk wit and humour for the first decade, or at least until some measure of genuine understanding has been gained.

For example, if an aged indigenous remnant is asked 'Have you lived here all your life?' and he replies like a shot 'No – not yit I hent!', he's not merely chasing a cheap chuckle at an innocent's expense but also underlining a deep and profound belief in his own significance as a fortunate member of God's Chosen Few.

This is a two-way street, of course, and members of the native population will have to heed certain guidelines as well if inroads are to be made into doubtful areas where distrust and deception have reigned far too long. They should be proud to be different, and for being blessed with the qualities that automatically bestows, but also capable of pulling up short of proving downright cussed and rude in the face of banal questions and stupefied looks.

An automatic resistance to change should not be written in stone, except where it clearly might have an adverse impact on what always seems to have been there. Remember the old Norfolk proverb: 'Progress is fine – just as long as it doesn't change anything.'

Jokes about furriners, missionaries, unscrupulous estate agents, Received Pronunciation, rich second-homers and planning gains should be kept firmly under wraps until a clear rapport has been developed. Pub conversations would do well to avoid all reference to 'them what move in and try to take over'.

In short, natives have to accept that newcomers and visitors – called 'blow-ins and grockles' in one to two ungracious quarters – may never grasp the full glories of the dialect and its humour, but that should never be used to score cheap points. Except in the village pantomime.

If the pub landlord or landlady happen to be recent recruits to the Norfolk ranks locals should tread softly and be sparing with favourite lines about how much better the place used to be before thatched space invaders and soup-in-a-basket. The pub remains a key player in the battle to brew up fonder relations between old and new.

Similarly, Norfolk's enviable array of splendid churches and chapels, many of them singing ancient hymns to open countryside, must embrace more modern ways of praise. Blessed are the incomers for they shall clap in the aisles, rejoice in the pews and laugh at the ancient verger's best line about taking 'Holy Commotion'.

There are plenty of helpful suggestions concerning other areas in the latest Norfolk Independence Party manifesto launched by leader Kirby Cane, former education spokesman, and his deputy, Lt Col Stratton Strawless, elder statesman and defence spokesman who favours a Nordelph Home Guard rather than a Ranworth Rapid Reaction Force independent of Nato. Other key figures in the hierarchy include Stan Hoe (agriculture), Doc King (health), Carleton Rode (transport), Pilson Green (environment), Lex Ham (culture and media), Wal Cott (sea defences), Dick le Burgh (ambassador to Southwold), Win Farthing (exchequer), Heather Sett (organic food) and Ched Grave (general secretary).

It is not my role to push the claims of this or any other party seeking power and influence in the county I cherish, but it is mighty hard to find fault with pledges to place Squit and Proper Joined-Up Writing on the Norfolk schools kerrickerlum, to legally empower village shops not to serve 'locals' who only call when snowdrifts block roads to supermarkets, and to keep the cost of bicycle tyres and inner tubes below the rate of inflation to encourage more environmentally friendly travel.

Just like anywhere else where 'vibrant development' can be taken for 'grotesque exploitation' and 'exciting prospects' for 'destructive juggernaut', dear old Norfolk has to sort out worthwhile wheat from choking chaff as the twenty-first century threshing tackle gathers steam. Perhaps the best hope rests in uncluttered sentiments expressed by an old Norfolk farm labourer many years ago before pressures and problems mounted so quickly and so obviously.

He peered across a familiar parish panorama he called home, morning sun washing the stubble of a freshly harvested field, contented cows ambling away from the milking shed and his bread and cheese and bottle of cold tea waiting for him under the hedge.

He turned to me, a reluctant harvest helper, and proclaimed with what now appears to be a terrible foresight, 'I dunt mind sharin' all this – but I'll be blowed if I give it away!'

୧୨

23 *Drinking it in...*

Tufty Thompson swallowed from the tankard presented to him by the darts club twenty years ago. He wiped the froth from his straggling moustache, pulled up the frayed collar of his old army coat and smiled straight ahead.

He'd heard it so many times, and he wasn't going to let them know if he was taking it in or not. Clifford, the bank clerk from Crab Apple Cottage, nudged his elbow.

'Trouble with you Tufty is you're living in the past. The war's over, old partner, and the horses have gone from the farms. And they harvest corn and sugar beet in different ways now. Modern techniques. We've all got flush toilets and electric light. No kids running about with the arse out of their trousers, and you don't have to use chicken bones to make soup for the rest of the week. And I haven't heard about one case of rickets since I moved into the village...'

Tufty heard but didn't listen. It'd be ringworm and six to a bedroom next. Bernard from the Old Smithy. Computer analyst. Squash fanatic. Wife makes her own jewellery, and advertises in the cottage industries section.

'Sad thing is you don't really mean it Tufty. You only hold on to those ration books in case a BBC 2 producer drops in to look for someone who remembers the good old days ... and that scythe in the shed hasn't seen daylight since Dick Joice started *Bygones*. And if you were so good at making your own entertainment, how come the Nissen hut fell down in a flurry of apathy in 1958?'

Tufty listened but didn't hear. Bound to be the magic of the local shop and the smell of freshly-baked bread out of the old kitchen oven coming up now. Graham the sales manager from Rosebank. Too busy and successful to get married. Doyen of the local dramatic society. Weekend rally driver.

'Come on Tufty, you could afford a modern suit if you had a mind. You dress like that so people'll buy you a pint. But the age of the Norfolk character is past … you wouldn't even get an audition for *Roots* if we decided to put it on. You resent us coming into your midst because we can see right through you. And that's nothing to do with your beloved malnutrition…'

Tufty neither listened nor heard. He saw Noel from Mill View breezing his way through to the bar. All curls and cigar smoke. Double-glazing business had to be good with three kids at the riding school. One of them had won a rosette last Saturday.

'Is it really true, Tufty? Your mother brought twelve of you up in a tied cottage? And you washed in a tin bath in front of the fire on a Friday night? How embarrassing when you couldn't find the towel when the club-book man knocked on the door and asked for three and sixpence, old money! And how did you all get on that charabanc for the Sunday School outing…!'

Bomber Brownlow asked for the tankard presented to him by the cricket club twenty-eight years ago. He smacked his lips in anticipation, hitched up his navy-blue overalls and set his cap at a jaunty angle as he smiled straight ahead.

Tufty listened and heard and shook his head with thanks as his tankard was swept away and refilled. Bomber, retired mole-catcher from Number 5, Back Lane Council Houses, put it a different way each night.

'Bludda sorft, lot on 'em. They wood ha' got a drink owt onus years ago if they hed ewsed wot theyre got fer brearns an' said we bort bit o'colour ter the plearse. Git it down onyer. Jist tyme fer wun moor … an yar tann ter bung!'

∽

Epilogue

A Norfolk countryman of eighty-five was asked by a holiday maker in August how he spent his time in the winter evenings. The old man answered, 'Oh, we make up a good fire in the kitchen an' then all sit round it torkin' about that rum lot what hev bin here durin' the summer.'

❦

A boastful American tourist said to Old Billy, 'Gee, back home we can erect a block of skyscrapers in about two weeks.'

Old Billy was ready for him. 'Blarst, bor, we kin beat that. I wuz on my way ter work th'uther day an' they'd jist started a'buildin' a row o'cottages.

'Time I wuz on my way hoom, they wuz sendin' the bailiffs in cors they got behind wi' the rent.'

❦

On his 100th birthday a Norfolk countryman was interviewed by a posh reporter from the city.

'Well, I suppose you have witnessed a great many radical changes in your time?'

'Yis,' came the reply, 'An' I hev opposed every bloomin' one onnem!'

❦

A stranger lost his way in the Norfolk countryside. He stopped to ask directions of a farmer putting up a small wooden building in his field.

After listening carefully the stranger then asked the farmer what he was building.

'Well, that orl depend,' came the reply. 'If I kin rent it out at a good price, thass a charmin' rustic cottage. If I can't, then thass a hen-house."

∾